An Emerging Dictionary
for the Gospel and Culture

An Emerging Dictionary for the Gospel and Culture
A Conversation from Augustine to Žižek

Leonard E. Hjalmarson

RESOURCE *Publications* • Eugene, Oregon

AN EMERGING DICTIONARY FOR THE GOSPEL AND CULTURE
A Conversation from Augustine to Žižek

Copyright © 2010 Leonard E. Hjalmarson. All rights reserved. Except for brief quotations in critical publications or reviews, no part of this book may be reproduced in any manner without prior written permission from the publisher. Write: Permissions, Wipf and Stock Publishers, 199 W. 8th Ave., Suite 3, Eugene, OR 97401.

Lyrics of Carrie Newcomer are reprinted with permission: © 2002 Carrie Newcomer. All rights reserved. From the album The Gathering of Spirits, available at www.carrienewcomer.com.

Peter Mayer's lyrics are also reprinted with permission. Visit http://petermayer.net/news/.

Resource Publications
An Imprint of Wipf and Stock Publishers
199 W. 8th Ave., Suite 3
Eugene, OR 97401

www.wipfandstock.com

ISBN 13: 978-1-60608-507-3

Manufactured in the U.S.A.

Contents

Acknowledgments / vii

Preface: An Emerging Dictionary for the Gospel and Culture / ix

A   Affections, Ancient, Apophatic, Attractional, and Saint Augustine / 1

B   Barth, Benedict, Bonhoeffer, Bosch, Bread, and Brueggemann / 9

C   Chaos, Communitas, Consumption, Conversation, Conversion, and Culture / 21

D   Dangerous, Différance, and Disciplines / 33

E   Ecology, Empire, Epistemology, and Exile / 40

F   Formation, Foster, Saint Francis, and Friendship / 50

G   Globalization, God, Google, Gospel, and Saint Gregory / 57

H   Heisenberg, Hermeneutics, and Hospitality / 69

I   Imago and Incarnation(al) / 76

J   Justice / 80

K   Kingdom and Kuhn / 82

L   L'avenir, Laity, Leadership, and Liminal / 86

M   Merton, Memory, Missional, and Mystery / 95

N   Narrative, Newbigin, New Monasticism, Notae, and Nouwen / 104

O   Obedience, Office (The), and Orthodoxy / 115

Contents

P   Paradox and Post-Christendom / 122

R   Rhythm and Rule / 129

S   Sacramental and Social Imaginary / 132

T   Theological Reflection and Theopoetics / 137

U   Uncertainty / 143

V   Virtue / 146

W   Webber, Williams, and Wright / 148

Z   Žižek / 156

Bibliography / 159

Acknowledgments

This project did not emerge from a blank slate or from the abstract and isolated musings of an individual, but rather chronicles a journey and a conversation. For the past seven years I have been immersed in a conversation that is occurring in books and articles, online in blogs and on forums, and at a variety of conferences and schools. I am struck by the diversity of people and groups engaged in this conversation around the gospel and culture. But perhaps I shouldn't be. The Spirit is hovering over the waters of what has become a chaotic world in transition. Something new will be born.

I have to directly acknowledge one contributor, who has also been a vital conversation partner. Apart from the friendship of Prodigal Kiwi Paul Fromont, I might never have taken an interest in Rowan Williams. Paul contributed the summary of his contribution, but has contributed to my own growth through his blogging, his personal journey, and his encouragement.

While I have never met Bruce Cockburn, his poetry and songs are rarely far from my mind. Bruce has been an invisible mentor. Several times in this document I use partial lines, and I would have used many more if I could have found the right source for permission.

Other conversation partners appear here, and some deserve special recognition. David Fitch has been a Barnabus, and his ability to straddle the worlds of the academy and the pastorate has been an inspiration. Moreover, his journey as a neo-Anabaptist leader has sometimes mirrored my own.

Alan Hirsch and Michael Frost, those crazy Aussies—through their books, talks, blogs and not a few emails—have also been inspiring. In particular Mike's talks at the Church Planting Congress in Calgary, Alberta in the fall of 2009 were tops.

There are so many others. Stan Biggs has been a constant conversation partner and a friend. My wife has been an inspiration, not so much in

Acknowledgments

the forming of ideas as in the constant and insistent practice of missional living. Her faithfulness to the king and her love for people kept my feet on the ground.

At another level of inspiration, Canadian singer-songwriter Steve Bell has been an unwitting partner in my walk with Jesus through these thirty-four years. His most recent album, *Devotion*, is possibly his best. But then my recent journey has involved a discovery of the richness of liturgical traditions, and Steve appears to be on the same road.

Finally, thanks to Cam Roxburgh, Anthony Brown, and Howard Lawrence at FORGE Canada. Your friendship and passion for the kingdom are inspiring.

The only way I can think of to close this kind of reflection is with an ancient prayer:

VENI, Sancte Spiritus,
reple tuorum corda fidelium,
et tui amoris in eis ignem accende.

COME, Holy Spirit,
fill the hearts of Thy faithful
and kindle in them the fire of Thy love.

Preface
An Emerging Dictionary for the Gospel and Culture

WHAT? ANOTHER DICTIONARY? And a proprietary one at that!

Or not really a dictionary, but a syllabus and anthology: a collection of thoughts, organized alphabetically by virtue of a particular conversation.

The idea for this project emerged, like so many great ideas, from a free-for-all conversation around breakfast one morning. We had a diverse group of people around the table, diverse in age, experience, and occupation, but with one thing in common: a passion for God and his kingdom. Later in the day I was reflecting on what made the conversation so engaging: it was both serious and playful at the same time. This delightful combination often seems to root a learning environment. I wondered how I could take that conversation and expand it, inviting others into a creative dialogue and into the learning process. I realized that our conversation had invoked any number of authors living and dead, and had spanned spirituality, leadership, education, philosophy, ecclesiology, and even cosmology. We had invoked Augustine and Barth, Jim Wallis and Dallas Willard, chaos, and culture. Someone had even shared a Buddhist koan! Really, one would need the most eclectic dictionary on earth! Why ... that's it. Why not a roving, eclectic dictionary that is both ridiculously current and particular, rooted in the broad conversation on culture, the gospel, and change; and at the same time, nearly universal, broadly inclusive, referencing names, old and new, that are used in this conversation? Why not write the ABCs of the emerging and missional conversation: an anthology organized by alphabet? In conception, this is *Wishful Thinking* (Buechner) meets *A for Abductive* (McLaren and Sweet) meets *Soul Survivor* (Yancey). And maybe there is just a touch of Brian McLaren in *A Generous Orthodoxy*.

Preface

The rules are simple: no more than five words per letter; names and personalities can occur on either side, attached to a definition or as referencing a word or concept; the tone is positive and constructive; and, while the overall interest is theological, the focus is life and mission—not theory.

So what would the first entries look like, and who and what would be included?

Under A would be *affections, ancient, apophatic,* and *attractional.* And of course, one would have to reference Saint Augustine. Augustine has never been more relevant, with his thoughts on desire beautifully elucidated by William Cavanaugh.[1] Augustine is the guy who quipped, *Inquietum est ad nostrum.* Those were his literal words, which in our clumsy manner come out as, 'Our hearts are restless 'til they find rest in you.' In our consumer culture, desire itself has become a commodity.

Some other names attached to these A words would be Robert Webber, Frost and Hirsch, Reggie McNeal, Jonathan Edwards, and Saint Gregory. Both Augustine and Saint Gregory are referenced in relation to the rediscovery of apophatic prayer, and the exploding interest in spiritual formation and ancient practices.

Under B would be Barth, Saint Benedict, Bread, and Walter Brueggemann. While Barth isn't an everyday name in the conversation around the gospel and culture, I am often struck by the echoes of his teaching around the recovery of wonder, or related to ideas like chastened rationality. As for Saint Benedict, the growing interest in missional orders can be traced back to his rule, and a very recent book[2] explores the vows of stability, conversion, and obedience with reference to renewal and missional engagement.

Bread symbolizes for me the rediscovery of a sacramental perspective and the renewed awareness that God is involved in all of life, especially the most ordinary things. But at the same time, it reminds me that the heart of memory for Christians is Eucharistic, and that most political celebration is always subversive. Walter Brueggemann is the *de facto* prophet of subversion, the poet who speaks against a prose-flattened world, and he will be found more than a few times in this emerging dictionary of the gospel and culture.

1. Cavanaugh, *Being Consumed.*
2. Cron, *Chasing Francis.*

Preface

Under C will be found *chaos, consumption, conversation, conversion,* and *culture*. What else? Chaos Theory was born in 1961 when meteorologist Edward Lorenz stumbled across a system that had sensitive dependence on initial conditions, making it impossible to predict outcomes. Even infinitesimally small variables can impact final results; the classic "butterfly effect." And in terms of the gospel and culture we have to deal with both chaos and complexity.

The last word, culture, has been described as one of the most complex words in the English language, yet we use it frequently and assume that everyone understands what we mean by it. Other names referenced here will be Jim Wallis, William Cavanaugh, Rodney Clapp, Brian McLaren, and Simone Weil. Weil said, "culture is that which forms attention."[3] Culture is a cultivating force.

Under D we take on *dangerous, disciplines,* and *différance*. The first word connects me to the cadence of Canadian songwriter Bruce Cockburn and his, "lovers in a dangerous time."[4] Love is always a risky venture, and should probably only be engaged when wearing seat belts and crash helmets. In a related movement, Walter Brueggemann reflects on the challenge of living as exiles, opining that, "We can only stand in readiness for what God may do . . . that standing requires the use of intentional disciplines that in every case are marked by danger."[5]

Well, you get the idea. Let's hoist the sails and set out, shall we? Who knows where the wind will take us?

---

3. Attributed to Weil, source unknown.
4. Bruce Cockburn, "Stealing Fire."
5. Brueggemann, *Cadences of Home*, 134.

Affections, Ancient, Apophatic, Attractional, and Saint Augustine

AFFECTIONS

In 1746, Jonathan Edwards penned his lengthy treatise *Concerning Religious Affections*. His interest, according to the introduction, was to explain how conversion to Christianity occurs. More specifically, he asked: "What are the distinguishing qualifications of those that are in favour with God," or, "what is the nature of true religion"?[1] In the revivalist atmosphere of his time, a heightened state of emotion was often claimed to prove conversion. It was abundantly clear that this was an unreliable way to discern conversion. A clue to his conclusions, and an echo of some solid current work like that of Alasdair MacIntyre,[2] is also found in the introduction. Edwards speaks of "the distinguishing notes of that virtue and holiness"[3] that are acceptable in the sight of God.

Much more recently, David Fitch[4] commented that worship in western churches tends to be organized around the production of experience. In this it takes one of two forms: the lecture hall and the rock concert (theatre?). The first setting is designed to stimulate thinking and personal reflection, and the latter is designed to produce feeling.

The lecture hall assumes an Enlightenment and Cartesian anthropology: Individuals are capable of acquiring truths through propositions and words, and this will somehow lead to transformation. Postmodernity,

1. Edwards, "Religious Affections."
2. MacIntyre, *After Virtue*.
3. Op Cit.
4. Fitch, *The Great Giveaway*.

Affections

however, has helped us deconstruct that pedagogy, and in the new culture Christians are constantly pummeled with images and symbols. All of these things form perception, form values, and shape thoughts and feelings. The hour-long sermon or lecture does not form us, and cannot adequately respond to the powerful enculturation, which the current generation experiences in a variety of settings day by day.

The rock concert and pep-rally setting is questioned because it is not generally shaped by a theology grounded in holiness, while at the same time the forces of culture industries act as technologies of desire. Meanwhile, in postmodernity there is no innate human experience and emotions are interpreted experience. Self and emotion are socially constructed based on power interests in a given culture (they want you to make the feeling connection between success and the girl and the new car!). Moreover, self-expression does not lead naturally to worship of God and can feed the illusion that self is at the center.

Fitch refers to "technologies of desire."[5] This phrase echoes the work of James K. A. Smith and the radical orthodoxy movement. Writing out of Foucault's insights into the nature of power, Smith notes that power is channelled through disciplinary mechanisms, and the goal of the forming power in western culture is to create good consumers. "By using repetition, images, and other strategies—all of which communicate in ways that are [transparent], marketing transforms us into the kind of persons who want to buy beer to have meaningful relationships, or buy a car to be respected."[6]

Smith notes that the primary appeal in all this is not to the intellect, but to the affections. It is not accidental that we are sold nearly everything we are sold in western culture through an appeal to sex or worth. Smith argues that in fact Hollywood and Victoria's Secret have it exactly right: *eros orders agape*. If this is true and represents a more biblical, incarnational, and holistic anthropology, then the response of the church is all wrong. The marketing industry accurately captures our will because it knows how to appeal to the body and the soul. "Victoria is in on Augustine's secret."[7] He continues,

---

5. Op Cit., 103.
6. Smith, *Who's Afraid of Postmodernism?* 105.
7. Smith, *Desiring the Kingdom*, 77.

Ancient

What if we approached this differently? What if we didn't see passion and desire as such as the problem, but rather sought to redirect it? What if we honored what the marketing industry has got right—that we are creatures primarily of love and desire—and then responded in kind with counter-measures that focus on our passions, not primarily on our thoughts or beliefs? What if the church began with an affirmation of our passional nature and then sought to redirect it? The result would be what Charles Williams called a "romantic theology."[8]

A romantic theology is a theology that respects integration and recognizes that the trajectory of the gospel is toward healing and wholeness. To recover wholeness we need to recover some lost voices and lost gifts: the poet, the prophet, the artist. Donald Goertz[9] writes that, "In the 21st century the artists will lead us. They are the ones who dream. Dreams and pragmatism are always in tension . . . God is always doing a new work . . . The artists help us to see it."

See also "Disciplines," "Epistemology," and "Postmodernity"

ANCIENT

That which is oldest is most young and most new. There is nothing so ancient and so dead as human novelty. The "latest" is always stillborn. What is really NEW is what was there all the time. I say, not what has repeated itself all the time; the really "new" is that which, at every moment, springs freshly into new existence. This newness never repeats itself. Yet it is so old it goes back to the earliest beginning. It is the very beginning itself, which speaks to us.[10]

The preacher opines: There is nothing new under the sun, and we begin with biblical warrant for finding the new in the old. And it was only a few years ago that the radio was blaring with Anne Murray's *Everything Old is New Again*.

One doesn't have to reach far to support that conclusion. 'New' monasticism recovers an old movement. Interest in Celtic faith expressions has probably never been stronger. And while all this smacks of faddish-

---

8. Ibid., 77.
9. Goertz, "Three Key Issues," 2.
10. Merton, *New Seeds of Contemplation*, 33.

ness, it also reveals a huge hunger for spirituality and spiritual practice. The hunger is evident across all social layers and in every culture, and it is evident outside the church as well as within it. The pragmatism of modernity has not fed our souls or encouraged depth in reflection, and our easy answers and quick fixes have only left us hungry for real and substantial fare.

The mystics, beginning with Saint Gregory, spoke of "compunction." The word was originally a medical term, and described acute attacks of pain. Translated into the spiritual life, it describes a pain in the soul that arises from two causes: sin and our hunger for God. Compunction is an act of the Spirit in us, an act by which God awakens us. This awakening is painful, like the thawing of a frozen limb, or the renewed use of a limb that is mortified. We are pierced by love and the attention of the soul is recalled to God.[11]

However, this is often a painful process and a living battle. How can that which is created of earth reach upward to heaven? This is an impossible task were it not for grace. A contemporary poet who has acknowledged the inner battle for the soul is Canadian Bruce Cockburn. In one of his early songs he sings, "*I've been touched by the beauty of jagged mountains . . . and cut by the love that flows like a fountain from God.*"[12]

There is something in contact with the divine that leaves an imprint on the soul. It is as if the soul tastes food that is exotic and unique, and is then spoiled for anything else. It is as if we touch a beauty beyond any we have ever known, and are never again satisfied. The bread that comes down from heaven creates a hunger that can be satisfied in no other way. We take the blue pill, and we are ruined forever. And this is a reasonable segue to apophatic.

Apophatic

In the west our churches are largely captive to culture. We box God and place him at our service, or market him as one more product for consumption. Pete Rollins' little book *How (Not) to Speak Of God* is an interesting response to this very modern position. While he doesn't frame

---

11. Leclercq, *The Love of Learning and the Desire for God.*
12. Bruce Cockburn, "Dancing in the Dragon's Jaws."

Apophatic

his response as apophatic or kataphatic, he nonetheless stands within the tradition of spiritual writers who describe both the presence and absence, the darkness and the light, in our experience of God.

Apophatic describes the *via negativa*, the journey to God through purgation. Instead of finding God in the light, we find him in thick darkness. This is necessary because while we deeply desire God, something else in us resists His will. We are broken vessels, and our very nature has been damaged by sin. We desire what we should not want, and we want what we should not desire.[13] Moreover, we continually seek to be the center of our own worlds and the principle of our own acts. We want to be like God, but we are not gods, and our attempt to sit on the throne of God makes us into devils. We seek to maintain our freedom, but end up ruling in hell.

God, however, in his mercy, doesn't leave us in this dismal and hopeless place. Instead, he begins the cooperative work in us of purifying our desires,[14] so that our desire and His become one. His goal is to turn our darkness into light, and to raise us to Himself, the source and goal of all life. That well-known mystic Saint John of the Cross describes the experience of the dark night of the soul. This experience of desolation, where God withdraws the sense of his presence to purify the soul of its reliance on feelings, is very present in Saint John's poetry. In the *Song of the Soul and the Bridegroom* Saint John writes,

> Where have You hidden Yourself,
> And abandoned me in my groaning, O my Beloved?
> You have fled like the hart,
> Having wounded me.
> I ran after You, crying; but You were gone.
> O shepherds, you who go
> Through the sheepcots up the hill,
> If you shall see Him
> Whom I love the most,
> Tell Him I languish, suffer, and die.[15]

This experience of the absence of God should remind us that we cannot manipulate the experience of His presence, nor should we try.

---

13. James 4:1–3.
14. James 1:2.
15. Christian Classics Ethereal Library, 1.

Attractional

This word appears to have been coined by Alan Hirsch and Michael Frost[16] and then made popular in their first book. They wrote: "The missional church is *incarnational*, not attractional, in its ecclesiology. By incarnational we mean it does not create sanctified spaces into which believers much come to encounter the gospel. Rather, the missional church disassembles itself and seeps into the cracks and crevices of a society in order to be Christ to those who don't yet know him."[17]

Later this came to be nuanced relative to "extractive." Gospel communities are attractive because they are places of love and acceptance and healing, islands of God's coming kingdom. But too often we have "extracted" new believers from their context and then cloistered them into safe spaces where they can learn and grow—but have no impact on their peers. Following Peterson's neat little translation of John 1:14, the missional-incarnational church is moving back into the neighbourhood.

In Christendom churches operated in an "if we build it, they will come" mode. This "come to us" style is rapidly failing, in favour of a missional "go to them" mandate. Instead of attempting to adjust the programs and services to please an unseen constituency, the effort is made to enter the world around us—an *incarnational* effort.

Somewhere Alan Roxburgh remarked on the false duality of attractional and incarnational. He made a good point. We don't want to stop gathering, and we ought to be *attractive*—the problem we generated by providing religious goods and services to a largely passive congregation and keeping this congregation busy in church programs was that we became *extractional*. We isolated and insulated people from their priestly involvement in their neighbourhoods. The fortress mentality of the western church is well documented and has too often been reinforced by the professional class of ministers.

Attractional is also not to be confused with strange attractors. These conditions result from certain characteristics of living systems that generate adaptation and dynamic life. Any system that is regenerating or grow-

---

16. Frost and Hirsch, *The Shaping of Things to Come*, 12.
17. Ibid., 12.

ing in a complex and challenging environment is likely to possess strange attractors.[18]

See "Incarnational"

AUGUSTINE, SAINT

His name appears everywhere. Whether reading historical theology, Luther, Calvin, or reading William Cavanaugh, Jamie Smith, Eugene Peterson, or Brian McLaren, one can't escape reference to this great African theologian. He is perhaps best known for his Confessions—a book that feels almost postmodern in its self-consciousness. The most widely quoted aphorism to survive is this: "You have made us for yourself, and our hearts are restless till they find their rest in you."

But why is Augustine so ubiquitous? And why now? First, because Augustine stood at the threshold between one world and another, much as we do. Graham Ward comments.

> It seems to me we stand, culturally, in a certain relation to Augustine's thinking . . . Poised as he was on the threshold between radical pluralism (which he called paganism) and the rise of Christendom, we stand on the other side of that history: at the end of Christendom and the re-emergence of radical (as distinct from liberal) pluralism.[19]

Secondly, Augustine's time knew nothing of the distinction we live with between the sacred and the secular. His worldview was not contaminated by this falsity. For Augustine there is no secular, non-religious sphere: We who stand in this post-secular space of postmodernity benefit by his perspective and clarity. And the theological foundations he was building suddenly make more sense that they ever made in modernity.

There is one writer in particular who has underscored the importance of Augustine's work for our time: William Cavanaugh. Cavanaugh is intent on critiquing the forming power of culture. Western market culture

---

18. Pascale et al., *Surfing the Edge of Chaos*, 72.

19. Smith, *Introducing Radical Orthodoxy*, 47. Similar to a comment made by MacIntrye at the close of *After Virtue*, 263.

is a profound solvent of discipline as of faith. Does Augustine offer us some resources to resist this shaping force?

Cavanaugh points to two insights from Augustine.[20] First, the meaning of freedom. At one time freedom meant freedom to pursue the good, but that meaning has gradually changed. Today freedom means freedom for my personal good: freedom to pursue whatever I want, without restraint or reference to any particular or transcendent end. So while there are true and false desires, apart from a clear *telos* (end) there is no way to judge between them. Second, the connection to desire and to its end. The key to true freedom is not just following our desires, but cultivating the right desires. The movement of our will is not in itself freedom: we must also consider the end to which the will is moved. Augustine points to the social nature of desire; it is organized by social forces. Cavanaugh quotes a spokesman for General Motors. The goal is "the organized creation of dissatisfaction."[21] Cavanaugh outright identifies consumption as a spiritual discipline. In other words, we are formed by market forces as good consumers.

These are helpful insights as we consider alternative practices and disciplines of resistance. One can go from here to some of the insights offered by Jamie Smith in *Who's Afraid of Postmodernism?* or the classical approach of Dallas Willard in *Spiritual Disciplines*.

See also "Consumerism"

---

20. Cavanaugh, *Being Consumed*.
21. Ibid., 17.

B

Barth, Benedict, Bonhoeffer, Bosch, Bread, and Brueggemann

Monastics have learned what Saint Benedict knew, and have in turn taught me, that real community is a gift, not something you construct. There is nearly everywhere today an intense, even desperate, longing to experience "I am because you are," and people are devising all sorts of schemes for 'building community.' The monastery is a living witness to the truth that community is something that happens when the environment is right, when hospitality is grounded in discipline and discernment, when prayer and work are rightly ordered. The Rule does not construct community: it hints at the conditions.[1]

BARTH, KARL

While Barth is not widely read and not widely visible in the emerging and missional conversations, his influence is everywhere. Barth recognized the need for adaptation and change when he gave guidance to a pastor in Marxist Germany in the 1950s:

> No, the church's existence does not always have to possess the same form in the future that it possessed in the past as though this were the only possible pattern.
>
> No, the continuance and victory of the cause of God which the Christian Church is to serve with her witness, is not unconditionally linked with the forms of existence which it has had until now.

---

1. Henry, *The Ironic Christian's Companion*, 149.

> Yes, the hour may strike, and perhaps has already struck when God, to our discomfiture, but to his glory and for the salvation of mankind, will put an end to this mode of existence because it lacks integrity.
>
> Yes, it could be our duty to free ourselves inwardly from our dependency on that mode of existence even while it still lasts. Indeed, on the assumption that it may one day entirely disappear, we should look about us for new ventures in new directions.
>
> Yes, as the Church of God we may depend on it that if only we are attentive, God will show us such new ways as we can hardly anticipate now. And as the people who are bound to God, we may even now claim unconquerably security for ourselves through him. For his name is above all names . . .[2]

Barth recognized that Christendom[3] was a compromise. Moreover, he recognized that while the forms of the church are fluid, its functions are unchanging. And unlike his contemporaries (and many others today), he did not confuse or conflate the church and the kingdom. The church in her institutional form is a human structure: limited, fallible, and contingent. Barth was able to love the church while maintaining an aloofness toward any particular embodiment or any particular structure or leader. Having lived through WWI and then watching the rise of Nazism before WWII, Barth was not naïve about sin and human nature.

I think that Barth would have understood the postmodern condition all too well. The work of theologians like John Franke or Stanley Grenz evidence a chastened rationality in light of the human condition. Franke writes that,

> Westphal suggests that postmodern theory, with respect to hermeneutical philosophy, may be properly appropriated for the task of explicitly Christian thought on theological grounds: The hermeneutics of finitude is a meditation on the meaning of human cre-

---

2. Barth, "Letter to a Pastor."

3. I am using the term Christendom to represent the ideological mainstream of thought as systematized and institutionalized in our culture, as opposed to Christianity, which I take to be the movement that Jesus initiated. Christendom has been the dominant religious force in the world for 1,700 years. Under Constantine Christianity moved from a subversive, marginalized and persecuted movement to "a religious institution with its attendant structures, priesthood and sacraments." For more on this see Murray, *Post-Christendom*.

atedness, and the hermeneutics of suspicion is a meditation on the meaning of human fallenness.[4]

At the same time, Barth was already moving beyond Enlightenment dualism. In this he anticipated the post-secular age we are entering. He did not view history as sacred and secular, and he understood the implications of that dichotomy for mission. Todd Hiestand writes,

> what I instinctively learned ... [was] ...World history was somehow profane and corrupted and biblical history was holy and redemptive. But, Barth shows that this dichotomized view of history is unhelpful to mission. The church would be "guilty of a lack of faith and discernment if it seriously saw and understood world history as secular or profane history." Instead, he states that we simply cannot separate the church from world history. He writes, "[The church's] history takes place as surrounded by the history of the cosmos and is everywhere affected and determined by it. Conversely, it is not without significance for the cosmos and its history that its own history takes place."[5]

Benedict, Saint

Jonathan Wilson-Hartgrove relates a story from John Alexander, for many years the pastor of the Church of the Sojourners in Washington, DC.

> Suppose a white person went to Arizona for a weekend and came back saying he'd become an Apache. He still talked the same, he still lived in the same place, he still related to nature the same way, he still talked to everyone he saw, and he didn't spend much time with Apaches. The only change you could see was that he wore buckskin Sunday mornings and went around telling people he'd become an Apache.
> What would you think? I'd think it was odd. I'd suspect he hadn't joined the Apache tribe in any meaningful sense.[6]

We don't usually think of conversion as joining a tribe. Jonathan notes that there is little evidence that American Christians actually be-

---

4. Franke, "*Reforming Theology*," 13.
5. Hiestand, "The Gospel and the God-Forsaken," 6.
6. Stock et al., *Inhabiting the Church*, 48.

lieve that the gospel offers us a new culture—a new identity amidst the multi-cultural sea.

The point was that culture is not learned or adopted in a weekend. It takes commitment to a people and a place—it takes time and life energy to become a Christ follower. Saint Benedict realized this, and it was part of his genius. Saint Benedict created a rhythm or rule of life around three vows: stability, conversion, and obedience. And then he created an apprenticeship called a *novitiate*. He understood that people could not simply decide to follow his rule. They would have to practice living it with others before they could understand what they were really choosing.

The three vows—conversion, stability, and obedience—are both anachronistic and appealing. They respond to the greatest solvents of our faith—the solvent of individualism is addressed by obedience and conversion, the solvent of formalism and Gnosticism is addressed by conversion and stability, and the solvent of fragmentation is addressed by stability and obedience. Saint Benedict's influence is everywhere, however transparent, and the meaning of discipleship, especially in terms of concrete practices, is explored by a variety of tribes throughout the emergent and missional cultures. This exploration is necessary because of the incredible fragmentation we now face, contributing also to loneliness. In part, this necessity rises from the loss of essential rhythms: the inward and outward rhythms of community and mission, work, and play, but also loss of the inward rhythms of silence and word found in a life of devotion. *Arhythmia* is a heart sickness, and often found where freedom is not rightly understood (see *Augustine*). Henri Nouwen writes,

> A Rule offers "creative boundaries within which God's loving presence can be recognized and celebrated." It does not prescribe but invite, it does not force but guide, it does not threaten but warn, it does not instill fear but points to love. In this it is a call to freedom, freedom to love.[7]

---

7. Northumbria Community.

BONHOEFFER, DIETRICH

Dietrich Bonhoeffer writes his brother Karl-Friedrick on the 14th of January, 1935,

> ... the restoration of the church will surely come only from a new type of monasticism which has nothing in common with the old but a complete lack of compromise in a life lived in accordance with the Sermon on the Mount in the discipleship of Christ. I think it is time to gather people together to do this.[8]

At the close of his landmark work, *After Virtue*, Alasdair MacIntyre calls for a new, though very different, Saint Benedict. Perhaps one of the personalities he hoped for had already appeared in the person of Bonhoeffer.

In a *Christianity Today* interview in 2008 with Richard Foster, Mark Galli asked what the most needed discipline in our day is. Foster answered "solitude,"[9] saying much about our culture, and reminding me that as we go out on mission we need to be anchored deeply in the life of God. Foster went on to say that he learned much from Bonhoeffer.

> I so appreciated in Bonhoeffer's *Life Together* the chapter, "The Day Alone," and the next chapter, "The Day Together." You can't be with people in a right way without being alone. And of course, you can't be alone unless you've learned to be with people. Solitude teaches us to live in the presence of God so that we can be with people in a way that helps them and does not manipulate them.[10]

It seems nearly impossible to spend much time in the missional conversation without running across Bonhoeffer. He is lauded by divergent groups, though most have some kind of tie with new monasticism. Like Barth, he stood prophetically on the margins of Christendom, and like Barth, he stood amidst the rubble of the Nazi empire and witnessed an alternate kingdom of justice, love, and brotherhood.

The relevance of Bonhoeffer, then, is that we too stand amidst the ruins of an empire. Increasingly our experience is exilic, and increasingly we stand on the margins. Our task is not to hope for a day when we can once again sit at the center, near the seat of power, but to simply grieve our

---

8. The Prayer Foundation, "Dietrich Bonhoeffer Pages," par. 1.
9. Galli, "A Life Formed in the Spirit," 3.
10. Ibid.

loss and embrace the humility of the suffering servant. As Robert Capon writes, "Marginality, in short, leaves the church free, if it is faithful, to cherish its absurdity; establishment just makes it fall in love all over again with the irrelevant respectability of the world's wisdom and power."[11]

In 1944, Bonhoeffer became embroiled in the plot to take Hitler's life (now memorialized in the movie thriller *Valkyrie*). On the day the attempt failed he wrote, in part:

> *Self-discipline*
> If you set out to seek freedom, you must learn before all things
> Mastery over sense and soul, lest your wayward desirings,
> Lest your undisciplined members lead you now this way, now that way.
> Chaste be your mind and your body, and subject to you and obedient,
> Serving solely to seek their appointed goal and objective.
> None learns the secret of freedom save only by way of control.[12]

Bosch, David

David Jacobus Bosch (December 13, 1929—April 15, 1992) was a member of the Dutch Reformed church, married to Annemie and author of *Transforming Mission: Paradigm Shifts in Theology of Mission*—a major work on post-colonial Christian mission.

Bosch was born in Kuruman, Cape Province, South Africa, and was raised in a nationalist Afrikaner home with little regard for his nation's black citizens. When the National Party came to power in 1948 and began implementing its program of apartheid, Bosch welcomed it. That same year Bosch began his studies in education at the University of Pretoria. Joining the Student Christian Association, Bosch had ample opportunity to meet black members of the community, and soon started to question the apartheid system. Sensing a call to mission, Bosch transferred to the department of theology. He graduated with a Bachelor's degree in theology and a Master's degree in languages (Afrikaans, Dutch, and German). He then went to Switzerland to study for his doctorate in the field of New Testament at the University of Basel, under Oscar Cullman.

---

11. Capon, *The Astonished Heart*, 12.
12. Bonhoeffer, "Stations on the Road to Freedom," 91.

In 1957, Bosch began a decade of planting churches in the Transkei. In 1967 he took up a position as lecturer in church history and missiology, training black church leaders in the Transkei. Bosch was concerned to bring good news to black Africans, and recognized that this could be confused with colonial and nationalistic motives that entrenched racial divisions. Bosch left his college in 1971 to become Professor of missiology at the University of South Africa in Pretoria, which at the time was South Africa's only inter-racial university.

In 1979 he helped coordinate a gathering of more than 5,000 African Christians from every background to demonstrate the church as an alternative community embodying the kingdom of God. In 1982 he promoted an open letter to the Dutch Reformed church, signed by more than 100 pastors and theologians, publicly condemning apartheid and calling on the church to unite with black churches.

Bosch wrote more than 150 journal articles and six books, including, *Transforming Mission: Paradigm Shifts in Theology of Mission*. The book was praised as groundbreaking by Hans Kung who called it the first book on mission to implement paradigm theory.[13] Lesslie Newbigin nominated it a new standard, a kind of *Summa Missiologica*. *Transforming Mission* surveys paradigms of mission both in the New Testament and through church history, highlighting that mission has always been shaped for good or ill by its context. Bosch then explored in detail what he saw as an emerging postmodern or postcolonial missionary practice, including one that is ecumenical and evangelical, incorporating a quest for justice and liberation.

Bosch labored extensively for a deeper biblical foundation for mission.[14] He lamented that the missionary movement had no consensus as to how the Bible functions as the authority, basis, and frame of reference for the church's missionary thought and practice. He advocated a rediscovery of the intrinsically missionary nature of the church, with the Bible as twin source: a standard by which the church understands its identity in Christ, as well as a source of paradigms and models for current missionary engagement.

Bosch sought to bring greater theological clarity to the meaning and relationship of mission and evangelism. He argued that any genuinely

---

13. As developed by Kuhn in *The Structure of Scientific Revolutions*.
14. See in particular, "The Structure of Mission: An Exposition of Matthew," 16–20.

Christian understanding of mission must reflect the wholeness of the gospel of Christ and the breadth of the biblical witness. "Mission," Bosch wrote, is "more than and different from recruitment to our brand of religion; it is alerting people to the universal reign of God."[15]

Mission takes place where the church, in its total involvement with the world, bears its testimony in the form of a servant, with reference to justice and salvation: the kingdom shalom of God. Evangelism is one essential dimension of that broad mission, the narrower concern to cross the frontier of unbelief with the announcement of the good news of Jesus Christ. Bosch summarized the church on mission like this:

> A community of people who, in the face of the tribulations they encounter, keep their eyes steadfastly on the reign of God by praying for its coming, by being its disciples, by proclaiming its presence, by working for peace and justice in the midst of hatred and oppression, and by looking and working toward God's liberating future.[16]

David Bosch died in a car accident on April 15, 1992 in South Africa at the age of 62.

Bread

In the literature and practice of missionality there are few things that feature more than hospitality, and at the center of hospitality is the table. Tables and eating appear prominently in the New Testament, where we frequently see Jesus eat with people. Later Paul writes to the early churches on generosity and the Eucharist, connecting the life of the body intimately to these things. We are one body, one loaf.

Few have noticed that this perspective will not permit a triumphal gospel. Nor does it fit with a gospel that is all about personal salvation because there is only one way to make wine, and only one way to make bread. Individual grapes are crushed, and individual grains are broken, and then heated or fermented to get a new life. In Christ we die, and in Christ we are made alive—there is no shortcut to the resurrection.

---

15. Bosch, *Believing in the Future*, 33.
16. Bosch, *Transforming Mission*, 54.

And all this calls us to a sacramental seeing where the divisions between sacred and secular disappear. In *Holy Now*[17], Peter Mayer describes a new way of seeing.

> When I was a boy, each week
> On Sunday, we would go to church
> And pay attention to the priest
> And he would read the Holy Word.
> And consecrate the holy bread
> And everyone would kneel and bow
> Today the only difference is
> Everything is holy now.
> Everything, everything,
> Everything is holy now.[18]

According to the Westminster Confession, a sacrament is the visible and outward sign of an inward and spiritual grace. But with the rise of the Enlightenment and reason, the possibility of a trans-empirical epistemology became increasingly absent. Increasingly, the world was distanced from God; transcendence and immanence grew further apart. The world was desacralized—split into realms of the sacred (heaven, the angels, and the numinous) and the secular (earth and humankind). Creation became *mere nature*—the realm where we work and play, not the realm of God's caring and immanent providence.

"Take, and eat. This is *my* body."

Distancing God from creation empowered the industrial age and the abuse of God's world. We lost more than the arts—we lost our soul. We forgot that we participate in redemption in this world and lost the ability to perceive God at work in culture . . . we lost the ability to see and hear Him at work in ordinary ways around us. Through the process of "objectification and analysis" we lost ourselves in relation to the world. We began to stand over against the world, an inevitable path to oppression. We claimed to seek understanding, but we would not "stand under." We became wise in our own eyes, and so foolish in the eyes of wisdom. Parker Palmer calls us to memory: to remember our connectedness to creation, and our call to care for the world God has made and loves; to understand our contingent and dependent position in relation to the Creator. In this call to humility is a call to transcendence:

17. Reprinted with permission from Peter Mayer.
18. Peter Mayer, "Holy Now."

> An education in transcendence, prepares us to see beyond appearances into the hidden realities of life—beyond facts into truth, beyond self-interest into compassion, beyond our flagging energies and nagging despairs into the love required to renew the community of creation.[19]

And so the most simple of things bears the stamp of incarnation, and carries our memories back to a simple table shared with friends. In the most ordinary of ways new life comes to us. Here we connect with the physical world, a corrective to our modern tendency to live in the realm of ideas. By virtue of eating bread and drinking wine we are reminded that salvation takes place in this ordinary world of sails and ships and sealing wax, cabbages, and kings.[20]

The grace of God comes to us in ordinary and surprising ways. God can speak in the gift of a child, the song of a bird, the rustle of the wind in the trees. The recovery of this way of seeing may hold more promise than we know. It may offer a way out of the polarized debate over the inspiration of scripture; it may offer a way to embrace a new wholeness in our living, and new possibilities for cultural engagement. Ultimately, it may offer us a more whole way of knowing ourselves, God, and our world. And all this because we gather around a simple table, a highly appropriate place for exiles.[21]

The shared meal is the center of our shared life as God's people because in sharing the meal we both proclaim and perform the gospel together. We become a sacrament and sign of the coming kingdom. And we are impelled into mission, because Jesus' life was poured out for the world. Walter Brueggemann writes,

> Precisely because of being broken and poured out, this bread and wine will never be fully accommodated to the interests of the old age. The world wants the bread unbroken and the wine still filling the cup. The world yearns for unrisking gods and transformed humanity. But in our eating and drinking at this table we know better. We will not have these subversive alternatives rendered void.[22]

---

19. Palmer, *To Know as We Are Known*, 13.
20. See the helpful discussion in Smith, *Desiring the Kingdom*, 199.
21. Frost offers a chapter on tables and hospitality in his book *Exiles*.
22. Brueggemann, "Covenant as a Subversive Paradigm," 1094.

BRUEGGEMANN, WALTER

When cultures collide, as modernity and postmodernity are currently doing, those who are caught in the explosion can feel that their world no longer makes sense. Old paradigms collapse, and the frame of meaning is lost. Those who thrive tend to be listeners and observers, and they join the process of communal searching and learn to ride the shock waves ... they contextualize meaning and discover a new way of making sense of the new world. They arrive at a liminal place ... a place between the two cultures where new possibilities arise. Liminal places are typical of all transitional spaces; they breed anxiety. They cause us to question our old identity, while failing to provide a new one. But they are powerfully creative places, places where the Spirit of God loves to dwell and to create.

Imagine the change that Jesus knew in emptying Himself of power, position and privilege. Imagine His real descent from glory and light into the world of darkness and dust. Talk about culture shock!

David's world was not so neat and tidy as our own. In Psalm 44 he writes,

> Get up, God! ... Are you going to sleep all day?
> Wake up! Don't you care what happens to us?
> Why do you bury your face in the pillow?
> Why pretend things are just fine with us?
> And here we are—flat on our faces in the dirt,
> held down with a boot on our necks.
> Get up and come to our rescue ...
> If you love us so much, Help us! (The Message)

So Walter Brueggemann writes,

> It is no wonder that the church has avoided these Psalms. They lead us into dangerous acknowledgement of how life really is. They lead us into the unthinkable presence of God where everything is not polite and civil. They cause us to think unthinkable thoughts and utter unutterable words. Perhaps worst, they lead us away from the comfortable religious claims of modernity in which everything is managed and controlled.[23]

Yet the spin doctors of the empire are not the only issue, the other issue is complexity and the pace at which we live. Increasingly we are

---

23. Brueggemann, *The Message of the Psalms*, 12.

content with sound bytes; the hundred and forty characters allowed on Twitter. Dwindling attention spans and information overload push us toward a phenomenon Noam Chomsky calls "concision," where complex issues are reduced to three points in three minutes, distorting reality and eliminating debate in favor of easy digestion.[24] It isn't only mass media that face this challenge. Pastors and teachers also need to recover a poetic vocation, refusing to reduce complex truth to three-point formulas, and refusing to narrow the gospel to four spiritual laws, organized around the small world of the self. Likewise we must refuse to reduce leadership to management and competency. We need to add a new leadership type within the apostolic and prophetic vocations: the poet.[25] The poet, like Adam, helps us make sense of our experience. The word in the prologue of John tells how Jesus "became flesh and lived among us." In a similar way, the poet shapes words so that what was hidden and invisible becomes known. Poets remove the veil and give language to what people are experiencing. This is only possible when the poet him/herself lives within the traditions and narratives of the people: "living reflexively in the traditions . . . The poet listens to the rhythms and meanings occurring beneath the surface.[26]" But the poet also has a prophetic bent: "Poets immerse themselves in the multiple stories running beneath the surface of the culture . . . feel the power of these stories and critique their claims and pretensions on the basis of the memory and tradition of the community."[27]

See also "Exile" and "Empire"

---

24. Wikipedia, "Noam Chomsky's Political Views," par. 18.
25. Roxburgh, *The Sky is Falling*, 164.
26. Ibid., 167.
27. Ibid., 165.

C

Chaos, Communitas, Consumption, Conversation, Conversion, and Culture

CANONICAL HOURS (*see "Office"*)

CHAOS

In the first chapter of the first book of the Bible we run into chaos. God has created, but the earth is formless and there is no life on it. But then the Spirit of God hovers over the water, and things begin to change. Order emerges from chaos under the active movement of the Spirit. Since that time the church has majored on order. "Let everything be done decently and in order"[1] might have been the watchword for ministry in the last generation. Run through a technological grid, we took this to the furthest point with church growth strategies. Prediction and control were the outcome of a scientific age and rationalism. We assumed that we had all the information we needed, and we assumed that the information we needed was nearly all quantifiable. Let's get on with the work, therefore, and build the kingdom. We probably should have been listening a little more to the book of Job (especially chapter thirty-eight and up).

Chaos theory was born in 1961 when meteorologist Edward Lorenz stumbled across a system that had sensitive dependence on initial conditions, making it impossible to predict outcomes. He discovered that even infinitesimally small variables can impact final results (the classic butterfly effect.) The outcome of all this was that the universe suddenly became

---

1. 1 Cor. 14:40.

much more mysterious, and we began to recognize our own hubris. A hermeneutic of finitude suddenly came back into play and large parts of the church began to rediscover mystery. Bruce Cockburn sings, "Can't tell me there is no mystery, it's everywhere I turn."[2]

In practical terms this means that much of the church is less fixated on outcomes than once it was, and less convinced that the things we can measure are really worth measuring. We are moving from fixation on the ABCs (attendance, buildings and cash) to more relational measures. Some, like Reg McNeal, have made a point of arguing that the scorecard has to change.[3] McNeal suggests that instead of asking: "How are our people doing," we ask: "How is the community around us doing"?[4] It's the kind of change that smacks of the Spirit of God hovering over the water, just waiting to bring order from chaos.

If we surf the edge of chaos for long enough, we will discover complexity. Complexity theory is not displacing systems theory, so much as moving it to a new level. Complexity considers the behavior of complex adaptive systems, like swarms of ants and a group adapting to radically new conditions. As a science, it represents three major steps beyond systems thinking:[5]

1. While systems thinking can address nonlinear events, it is rarely used to do so. In contrast, complexity science concerns itself with nonlinear effects where very small perturbations at the start lead to drastically different outcomes.

2. Complexity science is not build on the assumption that one can proactively control outcomes. Rather it emphasizes nimble reactions.

3. The living systems view conceptualizes the challenge of moving from point A to point B based on causal factors. Complexity concerns itself with the way the landscape itself changes as the organism moves across it: the journey is compared to walking on a trampoline. Each step alters the landscape.[6]

2. Bruce Cockburn, "Mystery."
3. McNeal, *Missional Renaissance*.
4. McNeal, *The Present Future*.
5. Pascale et al., *Surfing the Edge of Chaos*.
6. Ibid., 105–6.

COMPLEXITY (*see "Chaos"*)

COMMUNITAS

Turner's concept denoted intense feelings of social togetherness and belonging, often in connection with rituals. In *communitas*, people stand together outside society, and society is strengthened by this otherness. The concept is in many ways the opposite of Marx's alienation and is closely related to Durkheim's ideas about the sacred (versus the profane). *Communitas* as a social form alternates with "normal" social structure, and is, according to Turner's theories, not limited to the liminal phase in rites of passage. Many social phenomena are difficult to place within the rites of passage model of separation, liminality, and reintegration, but are more naturally considered a form of "anti-structure," alternating with normal social structure [as a dialectic].[7]

One way of understanding this dynamic is to view community on a sliding scale. What we typically describe as community is a convenient and voluntary association of sovereign individuals. Any meaningful bond is fragile and not very deep. However, when a human society or group comes under significant stress, it moves into liminality, and in that place the possibility of a new order exists: a *communitas*. For example, when the culture shifts and traditional roles are disembedded, we are thrown into liminality: anxiety and chaos ensue. People or societies in a liminal phase are a kind of institutional capsule or pocket, which contains the genes of the future. Throw away the sliding scale; this is closer to a cyclical process.

This may be ringing some bells, because it connects nicely to the work of stage theorists like Erikson, Fowler, and some of the work of Scott Peck. Peck[8] had a particular interest in community, and he described four stages in forming community: pseudo-community, chaos, emptiness, and community. Most groups, in Peck's view, hit the third stage and cycle back to the first, never achieving real community. But the promise of true community is enough to lead some groups further along the path. Moreover, in terms of transitional dynamics, *communitas* is the only way forward.

---

7. Turner, *The Ritual Process*.
8. Peck, *The Different Drum*.

When the landscape has changed drastically, simple adjustments are no longer possible. When we face escalating complexity, we don't have the option of engineering a new future. There are too many variables, and they operate and interact at a level that is beyond our ability to predict. In these places we need a radically new paradigm. If we enter a liminal place together, something new may be generated. Alan Roxburgh writes that,

> *Communitas* is a new kind of commons, an open space where we might discover and learn from one another in powerfully innovative ways ... The commons is an archaic, unfamiliar idea ... [it] refers to those spaces (land, ideas, values, relationships) open to ordinary people. They are collectively owned.[9]

This new commons is a place of both opportunity and danger. By definition it entails risk. It is Abraham hearing a call to a land he has not seen; it is Elijah in the cave; it is Joseph in captivity in Egypt. Alan Hirsch notes that liminality and *communitas* are strong elements in most adventure films.[10] Moreover, he recalls David Bosch: "strictly speaking one ought to say that the Church is always in a state of crisis [but] only occasionally aware of it."[11]

The potential is for something new to emerge: "*Communitas* is the willingness of people to risk entering a new commons where they journey together as God's pilgrim people in order to discern the future that God's Spirit might be bringing forward to them."[12]

See also "Notae"

CONSUMPTION

> Since Adam Smith, we have learned to assume that exponential growth is the basic law of economics and that no limits can be set to it. The result is that increased production has become an end in itself.[13]

---

9. Roxburgh, *The Sky is Falling*, 109.
10. Hirsch, *The Forgotten Ways*, 225.
11. Ibid., 226.
12. Roxburgh, Op Cit., 111.
13. Bellah et al., *Habits of the Heart*, 114.

Consumption

Churches are successfully turning out consumers rather than disciples. We've been asking the wrong questions for so long ("How do we retain our people?" or, "How do we grow this congregation?") that it's been tough to imagine the right questions. The dominant mode of the church in a market culture has been consumption, and to now change the scorecard inevitably means shrinking budgets and shrinking attendance. We are well trained as leaders to measure our own value by our ability to affect bottom lines, so the challenge we face is not only structural but personal. Who are we and what—or to whom—are we called anyway?

William Cavanaugh has done his homework with regard to the cultural milieu of consumption.[14] Cavanaugh notes that the problem with shopping is both its ability to create dissatisfaction with what we have, and its propensity to separate material things from their production. From there we arrive at our current culture where nearly everything is disposable. We know the price of everything, the value of nothing. In essence, our wanting takes precedence over our having. Cavanaugh rightly points out that nothing is wrong with tangible material goods *per se*, but it is the perpetual cycle of dissatisfaction and desire, and the quest to turn everything—and anyone—into a commodity, that is behind the problem of consumerism. Yes—shades of Noam Chomsky.[15]

Cavanaugh does a beautiful job of deconstructing the issue through the work of Saint Augustine. For Augustine, the first question is that of freedom. Relative to freedom, desire is not neutral. There are both true and false desires, but apart from a clear *telos* there is no way to judge between them. Here Cavanaugh recognizes the movement of western culture in the past two hundred years. Where once freedom was freedom to pursue the good, now freedom is defined as the ends that give me pleasure, clearly putting self and my personal good on the throne. The reframe I did not expect here was Cavanaugh's identification of the problem. Many people, under the influence of Buddhist thought, identify the problem as inordinate attachment. Cavanaugh says no, the problem is *detachment*.[16] This is rooted in the dualism we inherited from the Greeks, and the same dualism we quickly baptized via the Enlightenment and our resulting emphasis on an other-worldly salvation. The world is not my

---

14. Cavanaugh, *Being Consumed*.
15. Achbar, *Manufacturing Consent*.
16. Cavanaugh, *Being Consumed*.

Consumption

home: I'm just passing through. So what matter my stance toward possessions? Combine this position with a right understanding of suffering and we have a nasty stew: Yes, the poor and developing nations suffer in our market economy. But—they'll have their reward in the next life. We neatly absolve ourselves of responsibility on the one hand, while indulging our every personal desire on the other, with no engagement with the biblical call to "love justice."

But this problem of detachment is much larger and more nuanced, and its implications are profound. They relate to the fragmentation and mobility of our western world, our lack of stability, and our uprooting. We need to rediscover the theological category of land and its relation to covenant and creation. We need to become rooted in our neighborhoods as the place where God is at work. We need to quit commuting to gathering places across our towns where we are service-providers but not stakeholders, and become rooted and invested in where we live.

Cavanaugh outright identifies consumption as a spiritual discipline. In other words, we are *formed by market forces* as good consumers. He identifies two specific ways in which this occurs: in relation to transcendence and with regard to community. The counter-discipline he identifies is the Eucharist. Others, like Brian McLaren, suggest that our only possible response to the unholy Trinity of money, sex, and power is generosity, fasting, and prayer. Cavanaugh closes chapter two with this:

> We are not to cling to our things, but to use them for the sake of the common good. But to have a good relationship with others, it is necessary to have a proper relationship with things. We must understand where our things come from and how our things are produced. Things do not have personalities and lives of their own, but they are embedded in relationships of production and distribution that bring us into contact, for better or for worse, with other people's lives. A sacramental view of the world sees all things as part of God's good creation, potentials signs of the glory of God; things become less disposable, more filled with meaning.[17]

---

17. Ibid., 58.

CONVERSATION

Finnish sociologist Niklass Luhmann comments that community is a network of conversations. If there is a word that defines the phenomenon of emergence, and that characterizes the heart of the networks that are reflecting together on the gospel and culture, it is conversation. It must be, because conversation generates learning.

> Recently organizational theorists have been paying attention to conversation as the fuel of learning communities and the stuff by which organizations learn, adapt and change through shared knowledge. Since change is the order of the day, and since networks are increasingly important to us as we attempt to understand our world toward influencing change, conversation is inextricably linked to leadership.
>
> The most powerful organizational learning and collective knowledge sharing grows through informal relationships and personal networks—via working conversations in communities of practice.[18]

In the midst of rapid and discontinuous change, our old modes of engagement and frameworks for thinking about the gospel and culture are no longer effective. In effect, the landscape has changed, and the maps no longer describe the territory. Consequently, we have some unlearning and relearning to do, and this requires crossing traditional boundaries and generating conversations. Sally Morgenthaler quotes Surowiecki:[19]

> Groups that are too much alike find it harder to keep learning because each member is bringing less and less to the table. Homogeneous groups are great at doing what they do well, but they become progressively less able to investigate alternatives ... [They spend] too much time exploiting and not enough time exploring ... But, if you can assemble a diverse group of people who possess varying degrees of knowledge and insight, you're better off entrusting it with major decisions rather than leaving them in the hands of one or two people, no matter how smart those people are.[20]

---

18. Capra, "Creativity and Leadership in Learning Communities," 6.
19. Morgenthaler, "Leadership in a Flattened World."
20. Ibid., 175ff.

Conversation has the advantage of slowing us down. The pace of our culture is one of the challenges we face, because the faster we move the less we learn. When the pressure is on, when things are no longer working, we desire a quick fix; we want to rush forward. This is a choice generated by anxiety and fear.

Gary Nelson describes the people of Israel as they move across the Jordan into the promised land.[21] The ark of the covenant goes before them and it is set up in the middle of the river. God's presence—not our own skills or our courage—secures the ground. Moreover, Israel is not permitted to run ahead. We follow the leadership of the Lord.

But if one danger is to rush ahead, another is, "let's have another conversation." Nelson quotes Jonathan Wilson who argues for a third way, participating together in God's grace. We must reframe our attitudes and assumptions, listen to the Holy Spirit, and embrace the process at His pace. "Tomorrow the Lord will do wonders among you."[22]

The goal is to facilitate emergence. Once we could manage change because we understood and could control all the components of our systems. But with escalating complexity, this is no longer possible. Instead we have to surf the edge of chaos. This requires nurturing a network of conversations. Fritjof Capra writes that we must, "facilitate emergence by creating a learning culture, by encouraging continual questioning and rewarding innovation. In other words, leadership means creating conditions, rather than giving directions."[23]

See also "Leadership"

CONVERSION

What does it mean to repent? The word in the Scripture is *metanoia*, and it signifies a turning in both mind and heart. Conversion starts on the inside and works its way out. The word signifies a process more than an event. It means to keep on turning, to be renewed in our minds, to allow the light of God to expose new layers of our lives requiring a new sur-

---

21. Nelson, *Borderland Churches*, 31.
22. Ibid., 34.
23. Capra, *The Hidden Connections*, 111.

render day by day. Repentance—conversion—is an ongoing need for us as we follow Jesus. When our inner lives are exposed to the light we learn about the false self. That enables us to see it in others. When we live this way we can invite others along on the same journey. There is no "us" and "them" as if we have achieved something. We identify with the broken because we too are broken.

It is to Christ we are converted but not to Christ alone. *The church is the dating service—sometimes she thinks she is the date.* This confusion of the map for the territory, the journey for the destination, seems common in western culture. At the same time, conversion includes a communal element: when we repent of our sin and selfish ways we join a people on a journey toward wholeness, toward *shalom*.

In Hebrew repentance is signified by the word "shuv."[24] *Shuv* has a storied history—it pictures Israel returning from Babylon to be God's holy people in the land of promise. God gave to Israel the law—a code for living together as a political entity. So conversion begins with our personal orientation to God, but it doesn't stop there. It expresses a new *polis* in an alternate community under an alternate Lord. It embraces all of life, and in particular life in community.

What does this mean for life together with marginalized and homeless people?

It means that no one of us has arrived. We journey together to a land we have not seen. It means that together we learn new ways of being, ways that exclude no one. We build a new home together—a third culture and a third space that shows an alternate way of living in peace and friendship. As Stanley Evans wrote,

> There is only one way in which the church in the back streets can proclaim the Gospel effectively, and that is by action. The great mass of people have a very shrewd idea of what Christianity professes; but they have an equally shrewd idea that the practice of the Church in no way corresponds to these professions.[25]

We recognize we have all compromised in some way—we are all idolators. Western believers have been near the center of power for too long. Some of us idolize wealth and power, some independence or free-

---

24. Stock et al., *Inhabiting the Church*, 29.
25. Evans, *The Church in the Back Streets*, 35–36.

dom. Most of us are addicted at some level to culture, and we are all called to repentance. Gordon Cosby writes:

> Most of us are living, to some degree, as addicted persons, striving anxiously after power and money and prestige and relevance, trapped in the turbulence of wanting more. These addictions are so subtle for most of us that we have the illusion of being free people when in actuality we are immersed in society's expectations . . . We are subtle control freaks, truly believing we are turning our lives over to God but demanding a minimum of comforts.[26]

Control freaks, we sought to colonize other cultures with the gospel. We operated with a foundationalist ethos, certain that we brought everything there was of value, and that the host culture could teach us nothing. Conversion, then, was entirely on our terms and required a complete epistemological shift. The order was to believe, then to belong. But in the early church the order was reversed, and in this post-foundationalist era we are returning to belonging before believing. Conversion is joining a people on a journey more than it is accepting a set of propositions.[27] The gospel is once again becoming as relational as it was rational. As Bob Webber expressed it, "faith is participation in the truth embodied in the community."[28]

Culture

The last word, culture, has been described as one of the most complex words in the English language, yet we use it frequently and assume that everyone understands what we mean by it. The word cultivate shares the same root as the word culture. It is an agrarian metaphor, from the Latin root *cultivare*.[29] It means working with soil, caring for plants, animals, and the environment. We all exist in a particular soil, and we grow in response to the environment. The application is this: Culture is a cultivating process that forms people in a certain way. Culture is such a

---

26. Bailey, "The Journey Inward, Outward and Forward," 10.
27. See for example Condor, quoted in Belcher, *Deep Church* (85–86) or Webber, *The Younger Evangelicals*.
28. Webber, *The Younger Evangelicals*, 104.
29. Eagleton, *The Idea of Culture*.

powerful force, because it involves in an inward gaze that may be transparent to the individual. This transparency is represented by the Spanish philosopher Santayana, who wrote, "We don't know who discovered water, but we know it wasn't fish."[30] Culture is present through symbols like language and images, but it is also a lens through which we view the world of objects, things, people, and ideas: even culture itself. We create culture, and culture creates us. The complexity of this dialogical movement is well preserved in a statement attributed to Winston Churchill, "First we create our buildings, then our buildings create us."

I opened this book with a quote from William Cavanaugh. He writes that, "Consumer culture is one of the most powerful systems of formation in the contemporary world ... Such a powerful system is not morally neutral; it trains us to see the world in certain ways."[31] It does this primarily by offering a particular definition of humankind and our *telos:* our final destination. It tells us who we are, why we are here, and it defines the good life. Then it seeks to manufacture consent by a host of visible and invisible means, both social pressures and social practices.

When Jesus invited us to receive His love, He also called us to follow Him. When God's kingdom breaks into this world it encounters the false claims of other kingdoms, other lords. But if Jesus is Lord, then Caesar is not. The rulers of this world try to squeeze us into their mold.[32]

Should the church represent an alternative culture? Lesslie Newbigin offers us a clue:

> It is surely a fact of inexhaustible significance that what our Lord left behind Him was not a book, nor a creed, nor a system of thought, nor a rule of life, but a visible community. He committed the entire work of salvation to that community. It was not that a community gathered round an idea, so that the idea was primary and the community secondary. It was that a community called together by the deliberate choice of the Lord Himself, and re-created in Him, gradually sought—and is seeking—to make explicit who He is and what He has done. The actual community is primary; the understanding of what it is comes second.[33]

---

30. Attributed to philosopher George Santayana.
31. Cavanaugh, *Being Consumed,* 11.
32. Romans 12:1, 2.
33. Newbigin, *The Household of God,* 51.

Culture

Similarly, Hauerwas and Willimon, in the Preface to *Resident Aliens*, reference Philippians 3:20—our commonwealth is in heaven. They note that Moffat translates this word with greater force: We are a colony of heaven. A colony is a beachhead, an island of one culture in the midst of another. They write that the confessing church, "knows that its most credible form of witness, is the actual creation of a living, breathing, visible community of faith."[34]

---

34. Hauerwas and Willimon, *Resident Aliens*, 12.

Dangerous, Différance, and Disciplines

DAILY OFFICE (see "*Office*")

DANGEROUS

The first word connects us to the cadences of Canadian songwriter Bruce Cockburn and the poetry of his song *Lovers in a dangerous time*, referenced earlier. In a related movement, Walter Brueggemann reflects on the challenge of living as exiles, opining that, "We can only stand in readiness for what God may do, that standing requires the use of intentional disciplines that in every case are marked by danger."[1]

We live in dangerous times, and there is no escape.

We live in constant danger of accommodation to our culture. We live in danger of becoming merely consumers of religious services.

We live in danger of substituting the menu for the meal, the map for the territory, and worshipping the temple rather than God.

We live in danger of maintaining the values of the modern church, efficiency and success, and using technology to tweak the system instead of allowing the Lord to transform us.

We live in danger of suppressing diversity, receiving the plastic identity of offices and roles, and abandoning dependence on God in favour of security.

Finally, we live in danger of privatism and neglecting the poor, and failing to live authentically as a community of weakness and poverty.

---

1. Brueggemann, *Cadences of Home*, 134.

The challenge is to become lovers, even in these dangerous times. How will we get there?

The dynamic that defines our time is change. Change creates tremendous tensions and insecurities, but offers great opportunity. Where we can feel like strangers in a strange land, we also have the opportunity to reinvent ourselves from the biblical story, and connect in new and creative ways to that story and to the culture around us. Any time we are standing still we are moving backwards; life means change. As Saint Francis lay on his death-bed, he is said to have spoken to his brothers, "As yet we have done nothing. Let us begin again."

> A new church means reformulating the faith in radical ways in the midst of a community that has to begin again. For Ezra, as for Moses, new church starts do not aim at strategies for success, but at strategies for survival of an alternative community. What must survive is not simply the physical community; *what must survive is an alternative community*.[2]

Walter Brueggemann's work reaches toward a framework for survival for exiles. He concludes that the church model that dominated the modern experience was one that arose in the stable period of the Israelite monarchy, a relatively short period in Israel's history. The conditions that produced that model and made it workable were swept away in a cultural geo-political upheaval. That upheaval is not unlike that which we are experiencing in our own time. The model that has worked while Christian culture was dominant is now being swept away. There are signs of collapse everywhere. Even those who are not theologically reflective feel the tension and the cognitive dissonance. The western church is losing its connection with the culture, and where it most accommodated itself to the old culture it is most irrelevant.

Thankfully, the monarchical model is not the only model for the church. Brueggemann finds other models in the Old Testament, rooted in times of exile and transition and reflected in Isaiah, Jeremiah and in many of the psalms: 'How will we sing the Lord's song in a foreign land?' Even our familiar lands are rapidly becoming foreign to us; this is a time to rediscover that "we are strangers and aliens here . . ."[3]

2. Ibid., 108.
3. Heb. 11.

Dangerous

These are dangerous times because we are tempted to become so preoccupied with ourselves that we cannot step outside ourselves to re-think, re-imagine, and re-describe a larger reality. Brueggemann suggests that the stories of Joseph, Esther, and Daniel can guide us. They refuse to allow us to embrace any fundamentalist us-versus-the-world model, but seek to embrace "an endlessly cunning, risky process of negotiation."[4]

These are dangerous times because they require a shift in our self-understanding, and a "new" church means the end of the old one. A shift in self-understanding, however, only results from an identity crisis. Crisis and transition define the *chaordic* (ordered and chaotic) underpinnings of life in our times. A new self-understanding requires the most difficult kind of transition. Transitions are difficult because they begin with an ending, asking for a process of grief. Marriage is the end of singleness; a promotion is the end of a former job—and the routines and relationships that went along with it. You are not crazy for feeling disoriented and moody when you start in a new direction of faithfulness in Jesus. It isn't easy embracing insecurity. It isn't easy leaving our comfort zones, our titles, or our previous understanding behind. The goal is a living community we know that the home we seek has no professionals, only amateurs. Amati is Latin for lover and professionals tend to be hirelings who arrive with the baggage of identity and status. Only lovers will survive through dangerous times because lovers are rooted in the one who stands outside time, and who does not shift or change. Love knows a security that is founded in covenant relationship, and not in circumstance or position or performance. But identity is first a political issue: To whom will we bow? Whom do we worship?

This is why there will be few organizations that negotiate the transition. With bureaucracy there is always too much to protect, and too much at stake. There are too many established modes and means, and too many with titles and power unwilling to forsake them. There is too much demanded personally of the established leader when foundations are shaking.

When cultures collide, as modernity and postmodernity are currently doing, those who are caught in the explosion can feel that their world no longer makes sense. Old paradigms collapse, and the frame of meaning is lost. Those who thrive tend to be listeners and observers, and

---

4. Brueggemann, Op Cit., 11.

they join the process of communal searching and learn to ride the shock waves: They contextualize meaning and discover a new way of making sense of the new world. They arrive at a liminal place: a place between the two cultures where new possibilities arise.

Liminal places are typical of all transitional spaces; they breed anxiety. They cause us to question our old identity, while failing to provide solid new anchors. But they are powerfully creative places, places where the Spirit of God loves to rest and to speak.

See also "Brueggemann, Walter," "Exile," and "Liminal"

Différance

I've been reflecting on learning, leadership, and change, and a couple of images and ideas have been in my gaze. I've been wondering: What makes the difference? Why are some more inclined to listen, and to what are they tuned? Why the difference?

To be attuned to anything is to exclude other things. There is a connection between leadership and difference. Furthermore, to notice difference one must be in some sense on the margins. Indeed,

> Edges are important to life: in fact, we are drawn to them. They define a frontier that tells us we are about to venture father than we have ever gone before. "As long as one operates in the middle of things," states science writer William Thompson, "one can never really know the nature in which one moves."
>
> The visual cortex of our brain directs our eyes to look for edges, helping us to distinguish figure from background and consequently get our bearings.[5]

Now you may be hearing echoes of others who ran along this track for a time. The first is Gregory Bateson and his reflections on information: "information is difference that makes a difference."[6] If there is no difference, then information doesn't inform: it is merely noise. The second one who ran along a parallel track is Jacques Derrida. He coined a new word: *différance*. He notes that *différance* is neither a word, nor a con-

---

5. Pascale et al., *Surfing the Edge of Chaos*, 67.
6. Wikipedia, "Gregory Bateson," par. 5.

cept. According to Derrida, words and concepts are themselves *différance* from other words and concepts and this gives *différance* its meaning. That would give me the sense that *différance* is somehow transcendental: but Derrida denies this. Wikipedia explains like this:

> The word "house" derives its meaning more as a function of how it differs from "shed," "mansion," "hotel," "building," "hovel," "hours," "hows," "horse," etc. etc., than how the word "house" may be tied to a certain image of a traditional house. Not only are the differences between the words relevant here, but the differentials between the images signified are also covered by différance. Deferral also comes into play, as the words that occur following "house" in any expression will revise the meaning of that word, sometimes dramatically so.
>
> Thus, complete meaning is always *postponed* in language; there is never a moment when meaning is complete and total.[7]

If complete meaning is always postponed, it is always coming into being and never simply here or there. (Can you hear echoes of Jesus teaching on the kingdom of God?) Yet somehow listeners are tuned to difference, and perhaps to becoming. Change is somehow anchored in the future as much as in the present.

Disciplines

> Most of us are living, to some degree, as addicted persons, striving anxiously after power and money and prestige and relevance, trapped in the turbulence of wanting more. These addictions are so subtle for most of us that we have the illusion of being free people when in actuality we are immersed in society's expectations . . . We forget that Jesus, "though he was in the form of God, did not consider equality with God as something to be exploited, but emptied himself."[8]

The challenge is to break our addiction to the culture, even our addiction to church and temple. The recovery movement has taught us how to break free from addiction. We need supportive communities, friends who will

---

7. Wikipedia, "Différance," par. 2.
8. Bailey, "The Journey Inward, Outward, and Forward," 12.

hold our feet to the fire, who will love and encourage us as we seek to live out the disciplines of a committed life. We'll need the security of lovers, because the false powers that demand our allegiance and demand that we remain good consumers won't appreciate our resistance to the system. As we stand up for issues of justice, it will be obvious that our allegiance is to another King and not Caesar. If our values are shaped by Christ and by the teachings of His kingdom, we will increasingly feel like exiles in a strange land. Brueggemann notes that the response of exiles is shaped by Isaiah 40–55.

> Get you up to a high mountain,
> O Zion, herald of good news;
> lift up your voice with strength,
> O Jerusalem, herald of good news;
> lift it up, fear not;
> say to the cities of Judah,
> "Behold your God."
>
> How beautiful on the mountains
> are the feet of him who brings good news
> who publishes peace
> who brings good news of good,
> who publishes salvation,
> who says to Zion, "Your God reigns."[9]

As we deconstruct, and as we tentatively look for the presence of God in the desert regions, let's find a way to utter those subversive and liberating words. Because whatever we make of the current situation, we can't despair because our God reigns.

Brueggemann calls upon the use of intentional disciples of readiness.

- *Dangerous Memories* reaching all the way back to our father Abraham. Israel was tempted to substitute more respectable memories rather than embrace such messy stories.
- *Dangerous Criticism* that mocks the deadly empire. We must practice critical and reflective distance from our context. As in Isaiah, we need an ongoing religious critique of the tamed gods of the empire, and the political critique of entrenched power.

---

9. Brueggemann, *Cadences*, 118.

- *Dangerous Promises* that imagine a shift of power in the world. Assimilated exiles who accept the claims of the empire see it as an unmovable force. But this is idolatry. The faithfulness of God is new every morning.
- *Dangerous Songs* that predict unexpected newness of life. The people with dangerous criticism and dangerous promises gather to affirm a reality they have not fully experienced. As in the first century, worship is a political statement.
- *Dangerous Bread* free of all imperial ovens. The manna in the desert, the food of Daniel, the feeding of the five thousand, the recognition of Jesus when he broke the bread ... Certain kinds of bread enslave us, and others bring freedom. The empire does not control all the resources.
- *Dangerous Departures* of heart and body and mind, leavings undertaken in trust and obedience. Israel looked forward to a time of freedom from exile. Similarly, we need to imagine a time when we leave behind consumerism, competition and militarism for other territory.
- *Dangerous Acknowledgement* of how life really is. In the "glory" church that worships health and wealth it is easy to embrace a theology of the Spirit; less welcome is a theology of the Cross. But the kingdom of God opposes the comfortable religious claims of modernity where everything is neat and tidy, managed and controlled. Our God is good; but He is not safe.[10]

See also "Spiritual Formation"

---

10. Ibid., 118–33.

Ecology, Empire, Epistemology, and Exile

Ecology

Howard Snyder reminded us that our word ecology is related to the Greek word oikos (house) and *oikonomia* (economy).[1] The whole world is God's household, and his ordering of it is his economy. Snyder writes that, "Fundamentally, the Universe is not ordered logically, psychologically, nor sociologically, but ecologically."[2] Synder goes on to connect God's rule to *shalom*, an embracing metaphor. He continues,

> Will we opt for technology or ecology? This is not an either-or choice, but a question of dominant models. Will we view the world essentially as a machine or as a garden? Will we see the earth as a factory or as a home? Will we opt for technology or ecology? This is not an either-or choice but a question of dominant model . . . If the controlling reality is technosystem, mechanistic technology takes over and life suffers from being squeezed into the "clockwork orange" habitat for which it was never meant . . .[3]

The word economy is important in the New Testament. Ephesians 1:10, for example (oikonomia), describes God's plan for all creation. Christ is seated "in the heavenlies;" He is Lord of all. The church is called to manifest the first fruits of a plan of reconciliation, which extends to all creation, for "the whole earth is full of His glory." Redemption includes the liberation of creation from its bondage to futility.[4] The Christian, re-

1. Snyder, *Liberating the Church*, 56.
2. Ibid., 50.
3. Ibid., 43.
4. Rom. 8:19–22.

ceiving the inheritance of the Spirit and promised the world, is set free to let go of the drive for wealth and power: set free to serve.

The ordering of God's house extends to all creation. The Christian's role, then, is to be an oikonomos, a steward in God's house, extending the kingdom by incarnating Jesus' loving presence. The exegesis of Psalm eight in Hebrews two makes Christ the archetype for human dominion over nature. In the Old Testament psalm the point is made that the world is in humankinds' care. In Hebrews, Christ is identified as the Word of God through whom all things were created. He "upholds all things."[5] Christians are called to participate in Christ's role as sustainer of creation. This sense of connection to the land recalls many voices from the Old Testament. Land is the fourth most frequent occurring noun in the Old Testament, becoming a more dominant theme than even covenant. Elmer Martens points out that land has four theological dimensions: as promise, gift, blessing, and in relation to a specific life-style. Under this latter heading follow the questions of sabbath and jubilee.[6]

From Mount Sinai had come these words: "When you come into the land which I shall give you, the land shall keep a sabbath unto the LORD."[7] The text that follows points up two purposes: a religious one—to witness to God's ownership; and a humanitarian one—that the poor of the people may eat. Some scholars argue that Deuteronomy 15:1–3 couples a regulation about the release of all debts every seven years to the land's rest.

Elmer Martens points out that land, Yahweh, and Israel were bound together in covenant.[8] Richard Austin wrote that those who manage land are "tempted to create a sabbathless society in which land is never rested, debts are never cancelled, slaves are never released . . . and all of life can be reduced to a smoothly functioning machine. The powerful must resist this temptation, stop managing, and relax in openness to their community; then concerns for equity, justice, and mercy may come to the fore."[9]

Brazilians destroy massive tracts of Amazonia because it somehow represents for them the hope of a prosperous future. The forests of British Columbia fall for similar reasons. Overfishing, toxic waste, and the ir-

---

5. Col. 1:15–17.
6. Martens, *God's Design*, 108.
7. Lev. 25:2.
8. Op Cit. 97ff.
9. Austen, *Hope for the Land*.

retrievable loss of one hundred species a day: The welfare of the entire world hinges upon the land, but somehow the more immediate concerns about jobs and profits take precedence. In the words of a great native American, Chief Seathl, "we kidnap the earth from our children."[10] Land, then, is more than acreage or territory. It is a theological symbol, through which a series of messages are conveyed. It is the tangible fulfillment of the promise. Land is a gift from Yahweh, and Israel, through preoccupation with it, has her attention continually called to Yahweh. Land requires a specific and appropriate lifestyle. That land is real and spatially definable points to the wholeness and value of life in this world. Quality of life is all-embracing: relating to Yahweh, neighbor, and the environment. *Shalom* embraces all these meanings. The promise of land and all that it signifies keeps God's design firmly rooted in the world, and leads us to see the wholeness of the call to discipleship in the New Testament. In an eschatological frame, the importance of land is seen in that God promises to create not only a new heaven, but also a new earth.

Empire

In the signature song of his recent album, Bruce Cockburn sings, "possible futures all laid out/On the sweeping curve of the Interstate..."[11] The forces of empire mitigate against a theological reading of land or place. This amounts to a subversion of the gospel: an incarnation without a body. Similarly, an alternate reading of 'the good life' removes any sense of *telos*—of time moving toward a goal. The empire has a stake in removing any possibility of transcendence. But there is nothing new here. The word gospel was not first a Christian word. It was current when Jesus arrived on the scene in Galilee. The announcement of the birth of Octavian about 55 BC went like this:

> The providence which has ordered the whole of our life . . . has ordained the most perfect consummation for human life by giving it to [him] . . . and by sending in him, as it were, a savior for us and those who come after us, to make war to cease, to create peace

---

10. Hjalmarson, "Toward a Kingdom Theology," par. 18.
11. Bruce Cockburn, "Life Short, Call Now."

everywhere... The birthday of the god was the beginning for the world of the gospel that has come to men through him.[12]

Gospel was already a political term in Jesus' time—it meant the reign of a king who would bring peace, prosperity, and justice. He would maintain this peace by raw power through military might. The emperor thus defined justice, just as he defined the good life, promising prosperity and peace on his terms; terms which may look good from the inside, but which promise oppression and colonization to all who resist. In part, this is why Brian McLaren writes that the citizens of the kingdom are in rebellion "against the tyrannical trinity of money, sex, and power. Its citizens resist the occupation of this invisible Caesar through three categories of spiritual practice. First... generosity... second... prayer... finally... fasting."[13]

Brian Walsh and Sylvia Keesmaat take on globalization. They proclaim that what is really at stake is not merely production and consumption but "the construction of a homogenized global consumerist consciousness. Globalism wants more than your pocketbook, it wants your soul."[14]

> Globalization isn't just an aggressive stage in the history of capitalism. It is a religious movement of previously unheard-of proportions. Progress is its underlying myth, unlimited economic growth its foundational faith, the shopping mall (physical or online) its place of worship, consumerism its overriding image, "I'll have a Big Mac and fries," its ritual of initiation, and global domination its ultimate goal.[15]

Walter Brueggemann wrote that what we see in our western culture is a religion of immanence, always a feature of a civil and static religion.[16] The other two features are the economics of affluence and the politics of oppression. He finds these features in the transition of Israel from a theocracy to a monarchy, and in particular in the transition from David's rule to Solomon's, where God and the temple become a part of the royal landscape, in which the sovereignty of God is fully subordinated to the purpose of the king. From this point forward God is 'on call' and access

---

12. Dankes, *Jesus and the New Age*, 54.
13. McLaren, *The Secret Message of Jesus*, 70.
14. Walsh and Keesmaat, *Colossians Remixed*, 29.
15. Ibid., 30.
16. Brueggemann, *The Prophetic Imagination*, 28–29.

to him is controlled by the royal court. Brueggemann sees this as the final and deadly state of affairs after a long slide downward from the radical Mosaic vision of freedom and justice.

So what do we lose when we lose a sense of transcendence? The social purpose of a really transcendent God is "to have a court of appeal against the highest courts and orders of society around us . . ."[17] A second implication is the rebirth of hope for the future. Royal reality overpowers the dimension of hope and the place of imagination. When a nation (or a church subverted by empire) establishes a comfortable and static rule, the last thing they want is people with new ideas to shake things up. And in terms of the economics of affluence, you don't want people delaying gratification in favor of some future hope, you want them seeking pleasure in the eternal now. The result of all that pleasure is that in place of passion comes satiation. Brueggemann argues that one of the reasons we lose passion is precisely due to our success at achieving comfort and security. He states that, "Passion as the capacity and readiness to care and suffer, to die and to feel, is the enemy of imperial reality."[18]

How bizarre that the founder of our movement was crucified because he was a threat to the establishment, and then his movement itself became the means that anchored and protected that same establishment! We need to pray: "Your kingdom come." We ask for God's just reign to appear on earth—today—where we live and among us.

See also "Kingdom," "Globalization," and "Post-Christendom"

Epistemology

> Knowledge, too, is a covenantal affair insofar as it involves epistemic virtues such as humility and honesty and proceeds from an initial personal commitment.[19]

I was driving from somewhere to somewhere else when I was struck by the relationship of two words: *empire and empirical*. Empires in thought become empires of history. Framed positively, we hear this in Einstein's

17. Ibid., 29.
18. Ibid., 88.
19. Vanhoozer, "Pilgrim's Digress," 92.

Epistemology

famous comment: "the Empires of the future will be the Empires of the imagination." Here at the beginning of 2010 his words seem prophetic. Down in the dust of daily living, worldview and national myth seem to walk hand in hand. The stronger they become, the more likely they are to become oppressive hegemonies.[20] Not just what we know, *but the way we know*, is determined by ideologies, and the current Caesars usually have a huge stake in the way things are.

The dominant ways of knowing are one with the dominant culture. Epistemology becomes translated into an ethic. Since our primary way of knowing has been scientific, and since science divides the world into subject and object, inevitably our culture thrives on violence and oppression: violence against women, against the poor, against our environment, against those who are different from us. (The root meaning of objective is to oppose. Heidegger's calculative thinking versus meditative thinking helps us understand this difference.) Most of our knowledge is aimed at control.

But what if knowledge has less to do with mastery and more to do with openness? What if knowing is less rational than we supposed, and more relational: neither objective nor subjective, but personal? What would be the implications for the phenomenon of empire?

It's probably no coincidence that western civilization is in decline at the same time as we reexamine our assumptions around truth and knowledge. Together we are seeking a new way of faithfully living out the gospel, the full orbed gospel where Jesus, and not Caesar, is lord. I know that statement needs qualification: Every generation has sought to faithfully live the gospel. But few generations have had to undertake the journey we are making in these times, to reexamine our ways of knowing.[21] Parker Palmer wrote, "we must rediscover from our spiritual tradition the models and methods of knowing as an act of love."[22]

Our (thankfully waning) preference for quantitative over qualitative measures is not only a function of our technological society but a human preference for certainty, and an addiction to control. But the poets have long been warning us about the dark side of this preference. And in these

---

20. Foucault's critique of power, rooted in meta-narratives, comes to mind.
21. Tickle argues that this movement happens approximately every five hundred years. See *The Great Emergence*.
22. Palmer, *To Know as We Are Known*, 10–12.

times when "the center cannot hold," and so many things are falling apart, we should heed their warnings. Yeats writes,

> Turning and turning in the widening gyre
> The falcon cannot hear the falconer;
> Things fall apart; the centre cannot hold;
> Mere anarchy is loosed upon the world,
> The blood-dimmed tide is loosed, and everywhere
> The ceremony of innocence is drowned;
> The best lack all conviction, while the worst
> Are full of passionate intensity.[23]

When Heisenberg observed that the observer could know the position or the speed of the electron, but not both simultaneously, the world suddenly became a strange place.[24] But if our knowing was humbled, then we had the opportunity to kneel once more, and to bow in the face of mystery. Better still, we had the opportunity to recover an older approach to knowledge that did not promise control, but promised connection and a deeper knowing.

Amor est magis cognitivus quam cognitio. This old Latin phrase translates: We know things better through love than through knowledge. This brings us close to one of the oldest frameworks for thinking about spirituality, articulated first by Gregory of Nyssa. Gregory characterized growth in faith as entry into a moonlit desert night, then movement to a fog covered mountain, and finally into the impenetrable darkness of a thick cloud (Moses on the mountain). The more darkness faith could embrace, he thought, the greater the light it gave. This is classic *apophatic* expression, as compared to the more positive and *kataphatic* mode dominant in western churches. We need both perspectives if we are to honor the weakness and foolishness of the Cross.

> But God chose the foolish things of the world
> to shame the wise;
> God chose the weak things of the world
> to shame the strong.
>
> God chose the lowly things of
> this world and the despised things—
> and the things that are not—

---

23. Yeats, "The Second Coming."
24. Heisenberg, The Uncertainty Paper.

to nullify the things that are,
so that no one may boast before him.[25]

See also "Gregory, Saint"

Exile

The upheaval and dislocation that Israel experienced with the fall of Jerusalem and captivity in Babylon is not unlike that which we are experiencing in our own time. There are signs of collapse everywhere.

We aren't in Kansas anymore. A new world is birthing from the ruins of the old.

Barth tells a story about a series of lectures given in the postwar ruins of the Kurfursten castle in Bonn, Germany. In the summer of 1946 Barth began his lectures. Every morning at seven they met to "sing a psalm or a hymn to sheer us up."[26] By eight o'clock "the rebuilding of the quadrangle began to advertise itself in the rattle of an engine" as the engineers went to work to restore the ruins.[27] This is where vigorous theological work is always done, in the ruins of an old world with hope for a new.

Ripped out of the familiar world, Israel had to learn to sing the Lord's song in a foreign land. The temptation is to dwell in the past, in the glory days when there were predictable rhythms, adequate funds, respect in the wider community. When we lose this we feel frustrated, often angry, sometimes desperate.

Exile is not primarily geographic, but social. It is a place of liminality. The context of ministry has changed drastically, and thus our sense of identity in the community itself has shifted. A sense of irrelevance is common and ambiguity is now the norm. Expectations have changed and may be amorphous. Congregations are often living in the past, while those with vision are attempting to live in the new world.

Meanwhile, our beliefs about and images of the church are themselves in transition. The interplay of community and institution, organism and organization, formal and informal structures can be daunting. How

---

25. 1 Cor. 1:27–29.
26. Barth, *Dogmatics in Outline*, 7.
27. Ibid.

do we leverage the power of networks? How do we do discipleship in a consumer culture? Is the church a business or a community? We live with a duality where it seems to be both.

Relationships are critical. Theologically we prefer the communitarian and organic modes—but in practice modern churches operated like corporations. Leadership became an individual and lonely pursuit. We recognize the importance of relational modes, but seem unable to implement the best practices. Most leaders are aware of the dissonance of business models with the NT mandate, yet have been slow to jettison CEO type frameworks.

However difficult the exile was for Israel, it was a gift. It was an opportunity to rediscover God's call and his faithfulness. Yahweh was no tribal God and ruled even in Babylon. Theologically, the exile was a rich and creative time and many prophetic voices declared Yahweh's rule and spelled out his purposes.

Our parallel experience as we are pushed to the margins of culture offers a similar opportunity. The collapse of church culture offers the opportunity to re-imagine a faithful expression and challenges our idolatry and our pride. It offers us a way beyond the professionalization of ministry and *sola pastora* models that disenfranchise the *laos*.[28] We have work to do, and it is theological work; the alternative is to remain obsessed with data and technique. (And this is what the sociologists would predict. Ronald Wright's work on the history of progress has demonstrated that empires—like ideologies—always collapse inwardly via the dynamics of denial.)

In this new social location we can see the opposition of two gospels: one offered by Caesar, and another by Christ. The kingdoms of this world do offer real power and influence, at the cost of biblical faithfulness. The cross is replaced with the sword. But Jesus did not resist the power of empire, he absorbed it. Robert Capon writes, "Marginality, in short, leaves the church free, if it is faithful, to cherish its absurdity; establishment just makes it fall in love all over again with the irrelevant respectability of the world's wisdom and power."[29]

In the early church there were not many wise and not many rich. Historically, hope is born in the margins. Those in the margins have the

---

28. See Gibbs, *Leadership Next*.
29. Capon, *The Astonished Heart*, 64.

least to lose, and are the least tied to old modes and ways of being. They already lack respect. As a result, they are more ready to experiment, more prepared to follow into unknown lands. Ann Wilkinson-Hayes writes,

> We need to watch the margins of our society—the inner cities and the rural areas where creative approaches are emerging, often born in despair. And so when desperation forces us to let go of the old ways, God can bring new life.[30]

See also "Brueggemann, Walter"

---

30. Murray and Wilkinson-Hayes, *Hope from the Margins*, 18.

Formation, Foster, Saint Francis, and Friendship

FORMATION, SPIRITUAL

Richard Foster is not the only prominent living writer on spiritual formation, but shares the limelight with others like Dallas Willard. Willard defines spiritual formation:

> Spiritual formation, without regard to any specifically religious context or tradition, is the process by which the human spirit or will is given a definite "form" or character. It is a process that happens to everyone. The most despicable as well as the most admirable of persons have had a spiritual formation . . . Their spirits or hearts have been formed.[1]

Willard narrows the definition further by offering a specifically Christian interpretation: "Christian spiritual formation is the redemptive process of forming the inner human world so that it takes on the character of the inner being of Christ himself."[2] Willard clarifies that it is only in cooperation with the Holy Spirit that Christ is formed in us. The process is primarily a gift of grace, though it requires our effort also. He clarifies the role of disciplines and practices: "By 'disciplines' we understand consciously undertaken or chosen activities that enable us to do what we cannot do by direct effort."[3]

Elsewhere Brian McLaren takes up the issue of *practice*, using the analogies of art and sport. In the end, all disciplines are composed of practices that take us to places we can't reach directly. We do the scales so

1. Willard, *Renovation of the Heart*, 19.
2. Ibid., 22.
3. Willard, "Spiritual Disciplines," 107.

that one day we can play Bach or Mozart; we lift weights and run so that one day we can compete in a marathon. Brian's argument is that practice makes possible. He writes, "They say that practice makes perfect, but I wouldn't know about that. What I do know is that practice makes possible some things that otherwise would have been impossible."[4]

One of the gifts Willard brings to the arena of spiritual formation is his concern to recover a fully biblical anthropology. Moreover, he frames spiritual formation in a thoroughly incarnational worldview. Much of what has gone before has been Gnostic or dualistic: Willard understands that formation that aims at the spirit apart from the body—as though actual practice in this world is not important—is neither Christian nor forming.[5]

In 2003 Doug Pagitt published *Reimagining Spiritual Formation*. Pagitt was concerned to bring spiritual formation and the real world of bodily practice together. He structured his book on a weekly rhythm and described the physicality of worship as well as the need for the expressive arts.[6]

See also "Disciplines," "Incarnation," "Rule," and "Social Imaginary"

FOSTER, RICHARD

When *A Celebration of Discipline* appeared in 1978, a new conversation came into prominence. Where previously the conversation had been dominated by discipleship language, suddenly spiritual formation language had arrived.[7] But it wasn't just the language that shifted. Reg McNeal once said that if we want to change the culture, we must change the conversation. And while discipleship has always assumed certain disciplines, they hadn't been framed in this way. The title was evocative: a celebration of discipline. Could a discipline be something entered with joy? Could it be that freedom and discipline were not opposites after all?

---

4. McLaren, *Finding Our Way Again*, 87.
5. See in particular *Renovation of the Heart*.
6. Pagitt, *Reimagining Spiritual Formation*.
7. Foster, *A Celebration of Discipline*.

In the context of western individualism, Foster brought something subversive to the table.

Foster framed the disciplines in a way that made them accessible. These were not practices for saints who lived on mountaintops or in caves in the desert, but practices that enabled growth in faithfulness—formation in the spirit of Christ—for everyone.

Foster's classic divided the disciplines into three categories: inward disciplines, outward disciplines, and corporate disciplines. Four disciplines were listed under each category. In the introduction, Foster framed the practices as doorways to liberation—to freedom—thus taking on directly the perception that following the rhythm of a discipline somehow led away from freedom. For many people Foster's book was their first exposure to the classical disciplines and their first exposure to Foster himself. And who was this strange Quaker anyway, immersed in the literature and practice of the classical spiritual writers?

Foster's first book was shortly followed by a study guide, and then by *The Freedom of Simplicity*. Some years later the *Renovare* ministry was born. The website offers this definition of spiritual formation:

> We are all spiritual beings. We have physical bodies, but our lives are largely driven by an unseen part of us. There is an immaterial center in us that shapes the way we see the world and ourselves, directs the choices we make, and guides our actions. Our spirit is the most important part of who we are. And yet we rarely spend time developing our inner life. That's what spiritual formation is all about.
>
> Spiritual Formation is a process, but it is also a journey through which we open our hearts to a deeper connection with God. We are not bystanders in our spiritual lives, we are active participants with God, who is ever inviting us into relationship with him.[8]

Organized around a simple covenant, Renovare members make the following commitment:

---

8. Renovare, "What is Spiritual Formation"?

Francis

In utter dependence upon Jesus Christ as my ever living Savior, Teacher, Lord, and Friend, I will seek continual renewal through:

- Spiritual Exercises
- Spiritual Gifts
- Acts of Service[9]

See also "Willard, Dallas," "Rhythm," and "Rule"

FRANCIS, SAINT

> Praise be to Thee, my Lord, with all Thy creatures,
> Especially to my worshipful brother sun,
> The which lights up the day, and through him dost Thou brightness give;
> And beautiful is he and radiant with splendor great;
> Of Thee, most High, signification gives.[10]

Of the several poems which Saint Francis composed, the only one that has come down to us is the *Praises of the Creatures*, or, as it is commonly called, *The Canticle of the Sun*. The Canticle appears to have been composed toward the close of the year 1225 in a poor little hut near the Monastery of San Damiano. It may be the first work of literature to appear in the Italian language.

The Smithsonian Institute, while correlating one of the largest databases of writing on the planet, discovered that Saint Francis has been written about, cited, and referenced more than any other person on record. When Francesco Bernadoni responded to the mysterious calling of Christ on his life, he stepped out of the security of his family, the approval of his culture and even the safety of the church of his day. It was an obedience that led towards the darkness of the cross with only the hope and promise of the resurrection.

In an age of political and religious upheaval, an age eerily similar to our own, Francis chose a lifestyle that represented radical devotion to Christ, a literal response to the sermon on the mount. He cared for the

---

9. Ibid.
10. Sacred Texts, "Canticle of the Sun," par 7.

diseased in a time when medical care was virtually unavailable, accepting a painful death sentence on himself. Some scholars even believe that his stigmata were the wounds of leprosy. Whatever the explanation, it reflects his selfless embrace of Christ's sacrificial love.

The attraction of Francis endures and cuts across traditional lines of sacred and secular. Biographer Donald Spoto writes, "In the final analysis, this is what attracted me to Francis of Assisi—that he saw his journey to God as a process, a constant deepening and adjustment of his aspirations, a refinement of his presumptions about what God wanted and a winnowing of his own good intentions. In that regard, his conversion was not the event of a day but the work of a lifetime."[11]

A recent book stories the journey toward simplicity and renewal in the life of an American clergyman.[12] Tired of pursuing the latest fad, and beginning to suspect that success in spiritual terms looks much different than success as culturally defined, Chase Falson begins a pilgrimage to find his own soul and meets a ready mentor in Francis and his followers. The novel is not outstanding as a piece of literature, but it has captured a wide audience among Evangelicals.[13]

Saint Francis is the inspiration for more than one new expression of the church. He is the archetype of the holy fool, abandoning himself with wild joy in favor of a kingdom he has not seen, yet loves.

See also "New Monastic"

FRIENDSHIP

"The one thing truly worthwhile... is becoming God's friend."[14]

One of the most consistently powerful expressions of spiritual community is Christ-centered friendship. This is not friendship defined by a simple sharing of common interests, but rather a linking of hearts where two or more people covenant together for growth in grace (i.e., awareness of and response to God's presence and work in their lives). Historically,

---

11. Spoto, *Reluctant Saint*, 20.
12. Cron, *Chasing Francis*.
13. Ibid.
14. Saint Gregory of Nyssa, source unknown.

Friendship

some have referred to such transformative relationships as spiritual friendships.

Douglas Rumford defines a spiritual friendship as a Christ-centered, intentional relationship between at least two people, where these individuals focus on the nurture of each other's spiritual life.[15] David Benner adds more by defining spiritual friendship as "a gift of hospitality, presence and dialogue" given to another.[16] Benner sees the aim or task of spiritual friends as helping the parties involved "discern the presence, will and leading of the Spirit of God."[17] In these days of expressive individualism we tend to dilute our definition of friendship by making it contingent upon companionship and holding certain interests in common (e.g. similar hobbies, club allegiances, business, and social endeavors).

The great writer C. S. Lewis saw friendship as one of the four human loves, rich in its capacity to bring out the multifaceted beauty of God in an intimate circle of relationship among kindred souls. Lewis' language evokes something beyond hobbies to hint at shared passion and rich mutuality.

As we seek to develop meaningful, kindred relationships, perhaps one of the best starting places is to understand what's required in us ourselves to be this sort of friend to another. One of the most renowned ancient works on spiritual friendship is written by the monk Aelred of Rievaulx in the twelfth century. Aelred devoted much of his life to developing, modeling and encouraging transformative friendships. Here is his time-tested advice on the qualities needed in a spiritual friend:

> There are four qualities which must be tested in a friend: loyalty, right intention, discretion and patience, that you may entrust yourself to him securely. The "right intention," that he may expect nothing from your friendship except God and its natural good. "Discretion," that he may understand what is to be done in behalf of a friend, what is to be sought from a friend, what sufferings are to be endured for his sake, upon what good deeds he is to be congratulated; and, since we think that a friend should sometimes be corrected, he must know for what faults this should be done, as well as the manner, time, and the place. Finally, "patience" that he may not grieve when rebuked, or despise or hate the one inflicting

---

15. Rumford, *Soul Shaping*.
16. Benner, *Sacred Companions*, 46.
17. Ibid., 27.

the rebuke, and that he may not be unwilling to bear every adversity for the sake of his friend. There is nothing more praiseworthy in friendship than "loyalty," which seems to be its nurse and guardian ... A truly loyal friend sees nothing in his friend but his heart ... loyalty is hidden in prosperity, but conspicuous in adversity. A friend is tested ... Solomon says, "He that is a friend loves at all times, and a brother is proved in distress."[18]

We can look for people exhibiting these qualities (without getting overly idealistic) *and* we can work on becoming such loyal people ourselves.

Implicit in Aelred's listed qualities is commitment. True spiritual friends exhibit a high degree of intentionality in their relationship. It is that focus that makes spiritual friendship different from many other friendships: Two or more people are meeting for the expressed purpose of giving attention to their spiritual development. Dan Steigerwald writes, "This does not preclude simple companionship, but this relational connecting is supplemented by a greater desire to foster each other's spiritual development."[19]

---

18. Aelred of Rievaulx, *Spiritual Friendship*, 105–6. Aelred used Cicero's definition of friendship as a provisional working model: "Agreement on [all] matters human and divine, with charity and good will" where Aelred saw "good will" to mean a rational and voluntary choice to benefit someone, and by "charity" the enjoyment of our natural affection toward someone. Aelred dropped the "all" from Cicero's definition.

19. "Friends Practicing Attentiveness." Unpublished document shared with the author.

Globalization, God, Google, Gospel, and Saint Gregory

Globalization

As I thought about this entry, I remembered Genesis 11, the story of Babel, but I didn't immediately see the connection. It wasn't until I Googled it and found a talk by Dan Russ. Speaking of globalization and technology, Dan writes,

> I invite you to consider with me tonight the proposition that globalization, with all of its sophisticated complexities and potential enhancements, is, at the end of the day, a euphemism for technological imperialism which seeks to subjugate the diversity of humankind and to make it after the image of those who control the technology. In short, the internet, genetic engineering, robotics, and nanotechnology threaten to serve the primordial urge of human beings to play god in one another's lives: the same old garbage.[1]

Russ goes on to quote Robert Bellah, who noted that "Cultures are dramatic conversations about things that matter to their participants, and American culture is no exception."[2] Bellah suggests that there are four strands that comprise the cultural conversation that makes America: the biblical, the republican, the utilitarian, and the expressive individualistic. The latter two, according to Bellah have dominated the conversation, almost drowning out the republican voice and denying the legitimacy of the biblical voice. But all four are necessary.

---

1. Russ, "Babel." See also Walsh and Keesmaat in *Colossians Remixed*.
2. Bellah, *Habits of the Heart*, 27.

Globalization

Utopia, says the President of Nabisco Corporation, is "One world of homogeneous consumption."[3] It is not easy to embrace difference. What we do not understand, we fear. And fear drives us toward control. It isn't just the drive to acquire, but fear that drives globalization, an extension of the state project through its generalization across space.[4]

Babel is the story of humankind attempting in our own strength to create the city of God: a central place that is nowhere, that disregards both context and diversity to achieve power: the very spirit of technos.[5] Unity of language was not the problem; the problem was something within the heart of humankind, the same forces that are at work today in globalization. We seek to be our own gods, and we seek control for our own ends.

In the Genesis story God acts to restore the gift of diversity. And herein lies the promise of content creation and the worldwide web. The diversity of voice is simply amazing; there is openness, creativity, compassion, engagement, richness of insight, and often profound critical depth. It's the conversation that gives me hope, and I wonder if Bellah would today acknowledge that the republican and biblical voices have found new strength.

More than the conversation, it's the possibility of living an alternative story that gives me hope.[6] Formation—becoming biblical people—is a huge challenge in the face of an addictive culture that attracts us to the wrong things, and distracts us from the right things. We are not truly in-formed, because (a la Bateson[7]) largely there is no difference. But if there is diversity and difference, if the conversation becomes that creative commons, then perhaps this new lingua franca is a divine opportunity. So long as we can imagine the right things, God and His just rule, His king-

---

3. Quoted in Mander, "Eleven Inherent Rules of Corporate Behavior," 321.

4. See also the chapter in Cavanaugh, *Being Consumed,* and Ramachandra, Christian Witness in an Age of Globalization.

5. Some would say the spirit of megachurch or broadcast church or any ekklesial form that is decontextualized. See in particular the work of Jacques Ellul, *The Presence of the Kingdom* and *The Technological Society*.

6. Alan Hirsch writes in *The Forgotten Ways*, "Ivan Illich was once asked what did he think was the most radical way to change society; was it through violent revolution or gradual reform? He gave a careful answer. Neither. Rather, he suggested that if one wanted to change society, then one must tell an alternative story. Illich is right; we need to reframe our understandings though a different lens, an alternative story," 190.

7. Bateson coined the definition of information as "difference that makes a difference."

dom of shalom—so long as we can pursue the city that we have not seen, so long as we are walking toward God's future. So long as we are divinely discontent, then there is hope. As Norm Strauss sings, "There's beauty in the mystery/There's purpose in the waiting."[8]

See also "Empire," "Exile," and "Post-Christendom"

God

God is the subject of theology proper, and the Christian God has revealed Godself as a Trinity—an eternal communion of persons relating together in love. From the overflow of this love comes mission.

While it will seem odd to some, it is appropriate to root some thoughts on God in the question of language itself. According to Simone Weil, the function of language "is to express the relationship between things."[9] In our current cultural location, where the meta-narrative is suspect, we recognize that language is interpretive—it is situated. Yet language is all we have to share meaningfully our deeper experiences of God. When we grasp for the right words and expressions, we look for language that crosses barriers and that integrates the wisdom of head and heart. Poetic language functions to move us to the depth dimension.

The Brazilian theologian Rubem Alves reminds us that "Poetry is the language of what it is not possible to say."[10]

> There are words which grow out of ten thousand things and words which grow out of other words: endless . . . But there is a Word which emerges out of silence, the Word which is the beginning of the World. This Word cannot be produced. It is neither a child of our hands or of our thoughts. We have to wait in silence, till it makes itself heard: Advent . . . Grace.[11]

Our great mistake is to confuse the map for the territory. This is why when we do theology we must always both affirm and deny. The words we use are always pale analogies—only weak and limited servants for the

---

8. Norm Strauss, "Beauty in the Mystery."
9. Weil, *Gravity and Grace*, 3.
10. Alves, *The Poet, The Warrior, The Prophet*, 96.
11. Ibid., 3. Shades of Derrida, about whom more will be said under "H."

truth. They take us there, but they are not the there. With these disclaimers, let's consider God in Godself.

Trinity per se was a somewhat boring topic until recent years, the domain of dusty scholars probing esoteric mysteries. Perhaps for that reason it was neglected in favor of the sexier (and seemingly more relevant) Christology or Pneumatology. Consequently much of the church has functioned with a nominal monism—Christ is the real God and Jesus is the one to whom we relate and to whom we pray.

Douglas John Hall, a careful Trinitarian thinker, addressed this issue. He writes,

> I think that we can [recover a fundamental Christology] only if we recover a foundational Theology—a doctrine of God—that is informed by a Judaic sense of the dialectic of divine distance and proximity, otherness and sameness, transcendence and immanence. Christomonism and the exclusivity that attends it represents, I believe, a failure of Trinitarian theology. The result, in the hands of the simplifiers, is what H. Richard Niebuhr rightly named "a new unitarianism of the second person of the trinity"—or, in the plain and oft-repeated slogan of popular evangelicalism, the simple declaration: "Jesus is God." [This is] all the more conspicuously the case when our understanding of "Jesus," in the first place, is really a dogmatic reduction of his person, his "thou-ness," to the "it-ness" of Christological propositions that, most of them, enshrine little more than our own religious bid for authority.[12]

This is an emerging dictionary of the gospel and culture, so our interest here is the implications of a monistic lens—a weak Trinitiarism—for the recovery of the *missio Dei*. I believe that in part it is the recovery of Trinitarian theology that is rooting a recovery of good missiology.

There are several implications of neglecting a strong Trinitarian theology, and most of them are rooted in a skewed ontology.

First, we play into the individualism of western culture. Ontology has to do with *being*, and if Christ is all the God we need then God is not an eternal community of love. The work of the Spirit in creating a new humanity is thus in question, and we may be able to defend human potential as an individual pursuit. There is less reason to question the religion of self as the center of God's work in the world and the foundation of *missio Dei*—the overflow of Godself in love—is eroded.

---

12. Hall, "Confessing Christ in a Post-Christendom Context," 3–4.

God

Second, this reduced ontological center has implications for our sentness. Christ is sent and we are sent—a nice individual paradigm. But if Jesus' movement into the world is on his own accord as an individual, then mission is not a communitarian work of God and we too may go out as individuals to reap individual souls. There is no apologetic for a visible community as witness to the reconciling work of God. Yet more than ever, in a world increasingly distrustful of metanarratives, we need to see the peace of the gospel embodied in living communities. To perform the gospel is to proclaim it, or as Saint Francis is rumored to have quipped: "Preach the Gospel at all times; if necessary, use words."

Third, a reduced ontological center has implications for soteriology. Amos Yong has been building on the work of Clark Pinnock and others. He argues that when we start with Christology and soteriology, we have no basis for asking, "How is the Spirit active in other religions"?[13] (This is an inevitable subset of the question as to how the Spirit is active in the wider culture, and is one of the most pressing questions of our day).[14] Thus we retain the colonial stance that finds no value—and thus no meaningful dialogue—outside Christ.

But if we start with Pneumatology, and move to a Spirit-Christology, we affirm *de facto* a Trinitarian frame. Beginning with ontology we begin with our common humanity: a starting point *among* rather than above. We don't begin with the boundary questions that divide us and them; we don't have to prejudge and get caught in all the nasty disputes about who can be saved. Instead we move in the direction affirmed by Phyllis Tickle—toward questions of the nature of humanity and the imago. Then we are back with Newbigin on questions of prevenience and asking, "What is God doing in the world and how can we partner with him"?

Fourth, a reduced ontology forces us to a reduced epistemology. Instead of knowing by the Spirit and the word, we know by the word alone. This mitigates against a hermeneutic of finitude and pushes us back toward a modern scientific paradigm and toward objectivism. This foundationalist position is already in ruins.

Fifth, a reduced ontology will also reduce our epistemology. How we conceive being will impact how we conceive knowing. A reduced epistemology will tend toward a dualistic frame rather than recognizing that

---

13. Yong, "Discerning the Spirit(s) in the World of Religions."
14. Tickle, *The Great Emergence*.

knowledge involves both word and Spirit, is both cognitive and intuitive, and ultimately personal[15] or intersubjective. This failure has implications for our understanding and practice of spiritual formation.

First, that knowledge is rooted in love. What is not loved is not truly known, and this is true in the ultimate sense in relationality—the knowledge of one being in another. Secondly, because in Godself there is no separation between being and act. In Godself, contemplation and mission are one. This allows us to conceive of mission as prayer, and of prayer as mission, so that inward and outward life represents a rhythm in being. Indeed,

> God creates and missionizes from his overflowing fullness, freedom and love ... It is only in our relation to Christ, the God-man that, by Christ we become what we were created to be, viz. truly human. Moreover, we are also recreated to be "partakers of the divine nature" (2 Pet. 1:4), i.e., to participate in God's divine light, communicable holiness, and relational life through the energies of the Spirit. As holistic self-relation and relation with others proceed from our relation with God, so genuine human missions must arise from true contemplation. Prayer and missions are not in competition. "On the contrary," according to Jean Daniélou, "mission appears as the self-unfolding of contemplation."[16]

The best image we have of relationality within Godself is found in the ancient concept of *perichoresis*. The concept was originated by Gregory of Nanzianzus and is pictured as a dance. Clark Pinnock writes that, "the metaphor suggests moving around, making room, relating to one another without losing identity ... At the heart of this ontology is the mutuality and reciprocity among the Persons ... a circle of loving relationships."[17] The concept becomes a way of picturing an abundance of love that overflows in self-giving, inviting others into the dance.

> At the still point of the turning world. Neither flesh nor fleshless;
> Neither from nor towards; at the still point, there the dance is ... [18]

See also "Theo-Poetics"

---

15. See in particular the work of Polanyi, *The Tacit Dimension*.
16. Tan, "A Trinitarian Ontology of Missions."
17. Pinnock, *Flame of Love*, 39.
18. T. S. Eliot, "Burnt Norton, II," 22.

GOOGLE

Ten years ago, DVD players were still new, no one had ever heard of MySpace or Facebook, and there was no such thing as an iPod. Google came into being in 1998. And it was nearly ten years ago that web logs, or blogs, began to appear. I'm less interested in Google than in the way the Internet and web reality have changed the landscape by empowering participation. It wasn't so long ago that the "real" conversation around the gospel and culture was limited to professionals and academics, who carried on a running dialogue in books and journals.

The public and most visible conversation, however, was the one held by televangelists and TV preachers. Those who mastered the art of broadcasting claimed the largest spiritual, cultural, and political impact. Christian media consumption was a hit-driven business—fueled by mega-church pastors and best-selling authors. Those who could afford to play the expensive distribution channels of radio, television, and print controlled them, yet fewer than five percent of believers attended the large churches that supported this effort.[19] The Internet created a platform that eroded this apparent dominance. Small house churches now have the same electronic distribution channels as the biggest names from the biggest churches. Distribution—whether on YouTube or on blogs—is practically free, and so are the tools of content creation. Sermon podcasting, blogging, video streaming—all these venues for information and opinion are as ubiquitous as the Sunday bulletin.

What interests me is the Reformation dynamic present in Google, social networking, the Internet itself, and blogging. The first Reformation was empowered by new media. The new Reformation is similarly empowered, and more highly participatory than anyone could have anticipated. The impact on current theology and ecclesial practice is only beginning to be felt. There are many fundamental *loci* for that impact. One of them is our understanding of authority, and the second is our conception of leadership.

Blogging has other subversive tendencies. Until recently we all knelt at the altar of the professional leader.[20] In the modern world, knowledge

---

19. Suh, "Social Networking and the Long-Tail Church," 317.

20. See especially Roxburgh's summary of the evolution of the clergy in *Missional Church*.

was power. The man behind the podium with the amplified voice was its ultimate expression. With the fall of the idols of science, the contributions of Heisenberg and friends, we no longer slavishly trust the expert. Authority is increasingly tied to relationship: conversation, exchange, service, and time.

But if blogging and web reality subvert traditional views of authority, then we are all experts. Giving people a voice is a dangerous thing. Eventually they come to see that their opinions are as valid as everyone else's. Thankfully, they are mostly right. And when they are not, they quickly discover it. When we can go online and do a search for "covering" or "tithe" and read some careful research that contradicts the preacher, we gain a new level of freedom. When we can then discuss our discoveries with a group of other seekers, "authority" has shifted to an interpretive community.

That isn't a bad segue into a tilt at the topic of leadership. Could it be that leadership is less about the "hero" than about a communal process? Could it be that leadership is less about individual knowers and actors than about communal discernment? In his own take on leadership as process, Dwight Friesen observed that,

> Leadership is about conversation. Leadership has less to do with the clarity of vision, and much more do to with the quality of conversation. How one fosters conversation is everything: bringing self to the table, creating open space, speaking, naming, surrendering the need to be right, etc. Hidden agendas, unstated vision, passive aggressive needs to control, and rigid categories are just a few of the many ills ready to subvert [a learning] conversation.[21]

If community is a network of conversations, and if leadership is about conversation, then Google, blogs, social networking, and web realities are helping to facilitate leadership. This wider learning community is the seedbed for the future. Leadership is about change, and in particular about intervention (or destabilizing the system). Leadership . . . both

---

21. Friesen, 2. From this perspective, the best way to nurture community is to facilitate and sustain conversations. Organizational analysts Brown and Isaacs asked effective leaders to describe quality conversations. The characteristics were listed as a sense of mutual respect, taking time to talk and reflect on what is really important, listening even when there were differences, accepting and not judging the others in the conversation, exploring questions that mattered, developing a shared meaning that wasn't originally there.

Gospel

theory and practice in western ecclesial circles ... has been dangerously co-opted by the technological and managerial needs of the Industrial revolution.[22] We now need to move beyond command and control and hierarchical conceptions to theories and practice that embrace models of distributed knowledge and the complexity of adaptive systems.

See also "Chaos," "Conversation," and "Leadership"

Gospel

What is the gospel?[23] The shortest form is Jesus is Lord. Jesus is the good news, and He came preaching the kingdom of God. References to the gospel from many pulpits are reductionistic, as though the gospel can be compressed into three or four points, or dualistic, as if personal salvation can be separated from the advent of God's healing reign in the world.[24]

George Hunsberger comments that the verbs we use to describe God's reign, like extend or build, contrast with the New Testament verbs of receive and enter,[25] and thus point to a different kind of relationship between God's people and His reign.[26] Dallas Willard represents the dualistic perspective as the gospel of sin management. Willard comments,

> The Gospel is not that Jesus died on the cross for your sins so you can go to heaven when you die, but that the Gospel that Jesus preached was the Gospel of the Kingdom. When you say this to people they look at you like you're insane. "Of course the Gospel is that you can go to heaven when you die," they say. But the Gospel isn't a one-time event, it's a daily participation with Christ in the Kingdom life.[27]

---

22. A range of theorists and practitioners are sounding the alarm, including Lowney, Senge, Wheatley, Drucker, Houston, Peterson, McNeal, Sweet, Hirsch, and Roxburgh.

23. According to Wright, Paul's "announcement was that the crucified Jesus of Nazareth had been raised from the dead; that he was thereby proved to be Israel's Messiah; that he was thereby installed as the Lord of the world. Or, to put it yet more compactly: Jesus, the crucified and risen Messiah, is Lord." It is another way of saying this: "an announcement about the true God as opposed to the false gods." *What Paul Really Said.*

24. Bellah et al. *Habits of the Heart.*

25. Darrel, *Missional Church*, 93–94.

26. In this vein see also Ellul, *The False Presence of the Kingdom.*

27. Willard, "Stepping Into Community," 3.

Moreover, the church has sometimes been identified with God's reign, thus short circuiting the *missio Dei* in favor of church growth. Rather the church is spawned by the reign of God and directed toward it. The *ekklesia* is a sign and a foretaste of the *basiliea*, and an agent and instrument of God's reign.[28]

Western consumer culture has focused on the cross and substitutionary atonement. Clark Pinnock remarks[29] that we have fixated on the Cross in our thinking about the atonement, in part because we misread, "It is finished," and in part because western Christianity has focused on the legal aspects of justification over the experiential aspects (sanctification), placing the work of the Son over the work of the Spirit. In part this is due to the western focus on guilt over redemption: the walking out of the Christ life.

But the Cross is more than atonement, it is identification. And the cross is more than an ending; it inaugurates a new kingdom and a new community under a different Lord.[30] (See *Empire* above). Newbigin again, "It is surely a fact of inexhaustible significance that what our Lord left behind Him was not a book, nor a creed, nor a system of thought, nor a rule of life, but a visible community. He committed the entire work of salvation to that community."[31] There is no dualism in the gospel, such that salvation makes us nice people but doesn't affect the way we live with one another. Salvation is made visible—is an expression of shalom—when God reconciles us one to another. Hauerwas and Willimon write,

> The confessing church ... depicts that conversion as a long process of being baptismally engrafted into a new people, an alternative *polis*, a countercultural social structure called church. It seeks to influence the world by being the church, that is, by being something the world is not and can never be ... The confessing church seeks the visible church, a place, clearly visible to the world, in which people are faithful to their promises, love their enemies, tell the truth, honor the poor, suffer for righteousness, and thereby testify to the amazing community-creating power of God.[32]

---

28. Guder. Op Cit., 98–101.

29. Op Cit.

30. Thus John Driver asked, "The church is by definition a community. The question which confronts the church today therefore is, what kind of community will we be?"

31. Newbigin. *Household of God*.

32. Op Cit., 47.

Gregory

See also "Incarnation" and "Kingdom"

GREGORY, SAINT

Under "Epistemology" we referenced one of the oldest frameworks for thinking about spirituality, articulated by Gregory of Nyssa. Gregory speaks of three stages of spiritual growth, which progress from the darkness of ignorance, through spiritual illumination, and finally returns to a darkness of the mind in contemplation of a God who is Infinite in essence and therefore beyond our comprehension.

Gregory followed Philo in using the story of Moses as an allegory for spiritual life. When Moses first meets God in the burning bush God reveals himself, and even gives Moses his name. Later Moses meets God in the cloud and realizes that God cannot be seen by human eyes. Ascending Mount Sinai, Moses comes to a further knowledge of God and discovers that God is also beyond the human mind. Gregory is thus the father of paradox as a theological strain. It is only through not-knowing and not-seeing that God can, paradoxically, be known and seen. Later John of the Cross encapsulated this journey into faith in his spiritual songs. He wrote,

> This knowing that unknows
> has mastery so great,
> should any sage oppose
> he'd blunder in debate,
> being no such advocate
> as know not knowing there,
> burst the mind's barrier ...
>
> Souls beyond selfhood caught
> know, not knowing, there:
> burst the mind's barrier.[33]

Gregory is the major figure in what became known as the apophatic stream of spirituality—the way of negation, as opposed to the kataphatic—the way of affirmation. Gregory believed that the more darkness faith could embrace, the greater the light it would give.

---

33. Nims, *St. John of the Cross*, 27–29.

Gregory

This was a revolutionary perspective when set alongside the most common theological frames of the day. Plato still held great influence among classical thinkers, and was a major theological influence. Gregory advanced the idea of *epektasis*, or constant progress. He described the ideal of human perfection as constant progress in virtue and godliness. Our goal is to become more and more perfect, more like God, even though we will not attain God's transcendence.

These ideas are common in Christian spirituality today, and also connect to the epistemology of love, so prominent in the monastic writers. If the mind cannot know God directly, this remains no barrier to the soul. Love is the path to true knowledge, and the Spirit Himself pours the love of God into our hearts, enabling us to know God.

Love is a distinct kind of knowing. Somewhere Eugene Peterson writes about love that it is our first language, the language of attachment, but a language we often lose as we become instrumental and interested in effects. Most of us need to relearn the language of the heart to remain whole human beings. While we can know God with the mind, God is personal, and He is not fully known unless He is loved. The call to contemplation is the call to know God beyond our senses and beyond our intellect; to directly apprehend Him with our spirit so that deep calls to deep.

Pete Rollins picked up the apophatic stream and the necessity of paradox. He writes that "revelation ought not to be thought of either as that which makes God known or as that which leaves God unknown, but rather as the overpowering light that renders God known *as* unknown."[34] In many ways Rollins books comes to us in the ruins of modernity as a reminder of the limits of reason. Or, in the words of Westphal, "The hermeneutics of finitude is a meditation on the meaning of human createdness, and the hermeneutics of suspicion is a meditation on the meaning of human fallenness."[35]

See also "Epistemology," and "Mystery"

---

34. Rollins, *How (Not) to Speak of God*, 17.
35. As cited in Franke, "Reforming Theology," 13.

Heisenberg, Hermeneutics, and Hospitality

Heisenberg

> The more precisely the position is determined, the less precisely the momentum is known in this instant, and vice versa.[1]

This is a succinct statement of the uncertainty relation between the position and the momentum (mass times velocity) of a subatomic particle such as an electron. Heisenberg first advanced this proposition in the heady early days of quantum physics and the work of Einstein on relativity. The implications are no less profound today. The Newtonian world of cause and effect has become increasingly remote. Attempts to predict or control the behavior of complex systems have become a pipe dream: the legacy of a world that no longer exists.

Some sage has remarked that management is about stability; leadership is about change. We don't much about change, particularly in complex systems. The little we know is that there is rarely a one to one correspondence between our acts and the effects. In the post-Einstein world of Heisenberg and Schrödinger, in the world of probabilities and uncertainty, change is more a mystery than ever.

So, in between cause and effect is mystery. In between leadership and change is a shadow and a gap. In that place between the sea and the foam, we need spirituality. We need the ability to embrace mystery, and a level of comfort with paradox. We know that it is not our efforts that will bring the kingdom—that our part, while important, remains mysterious and small. We know that Oscar Romero was right. We know that Dag

---

1. Wikiquote, *Werner Heisenberg*.

Hermeneutics

Hammarskjöld was onto something. We know that Dame Julian was right when she said, "All manner of thing shall be well..."[2]

See also "Chaos," "Mystery," and "Uncertainty"

HERMENEUTICS

Stan Grenz sketched the contours of a postmodern gospel. He wrote that,

> Postmodern thinkers rightly alert us to the naiveté of the Enlightenment attempt to discover universal truth by appeal to reason alone. Ultimately the metanarrative we proclaim lies beyond the pale of reason to discover or to evaluate. Therefore, we agree that in this world we will witness the struggle among conflicting metanarratives and interpretations of reality. But we add that although all interpretations are in some sense invalid, they cannot all be *equally* invalid. We believe that conflicting interpretations can be evaluated according to a criterion that in some sense transcends them all. Because we believe that 'the Word became flesh' in Jesus Christ, we are convinced that this criterion is the story of God's action in Jesus of Nazareth.[3]

While interpretation may now be the order of the day, and while we may acknowledge that "all reality is scripted," or "authorized by a text,"[4] reality is still out there. Yes—we are situated. Yes—even language itself limits what we can say (echoes again of the tension between the *via negativa* and the *via positiva*). Reality is out there, revealed in Christ, so that we may acknowledge and confess that Jesus is Lord.

But that is perhaps moving too quickly over some seriously rugged terrain. Colin Greene writes that, "Scientific rationality and indeed the *prima philosophie* of the Enlightenment that sought to locate the foundations of knowledge in some epistemologically privileged aspect of human

---

2. These words of Julian of Norwich (*Showings*) picked up by Eliot in the closing lines of *Four Quartets*.
3. Grenz, *A Primer on Postmodernism*, 165.
4. Both these phrases in Brueggemann, *Cadences of Home*, 26–27.

subjectivity has given way to the linguistic and hermeneutical turn in modern cultural theory."[5]

This is a complex story, but philosophy professor John Caputo describes the landscape with humor and brevity. I will summarize one of the chapters in his excellent book here.[6]

Caputo describes three background ideas that shaped the postmodern situation. In *Being and Time* (1927) Martin Heidegger argued that as soon as we come to be we find that we are already there. We can never get outside our own skins, as if we could look down at ourselves from above. If there is a god's eye view, it belongs to God. We are shaped by the assumptions we inherit. It's true that everyone has an angle—but angles don't bend and distort, they give us access we would not otherwise have. The recognition of this situation is the *hermeneutical turn*.[7]

Secondly, when Descartes wrote the *Meditations*, he was already *writing*. In other words, one of the assumptions that Descartes missed when he put everything in doubt was that the entire work of doubt required language. The title he borrowed from his Jesuit teachers—*Meditations*—was meant to connote a pure seeing; a naked and even pre-linguistic contact with the soul. But everything he wrote was deeply colored by the language he inherited from his teachers. Language is a cultural entity, and like all cultural entities, it is deeply embedded in people and place. There is no such thing as a private language. We make progress in thinking not by shedding language for something else, but by finding new combinations of words, and more nuanced description. But this discovery that we are located by language and there is no escape is the linguistic turn.[8]

The final turn arrived with Thomas Kuhn. Writing as a scientist from the inside, Kuhn simply made the point that science itself is not passive observation, and not free of assumptions. In fact the opposite is true. Scientists work under overarching frameworks called paradigms, that allow them to organize their experiments (similar to the angles above). Once in a while they find information that fits no paradigm, and they are required to rethink the frameworks they work within. And while they may have discovered a deeper truth, inevitably the new framework is attacked

5. Greene, *Newbigin to Where?* 3.
6. Caputo, *Philosophy and Theology*, 44–49.
7. Ibid., 45.
8. Ibid., 46.

by the established scientists long before it is embraced. At the start of the revolution, all the evidence is on the side of the "old guard," and the young mavericks are running mostly on intuition. By the end of the revolution the evidence is on the side of the new. The point is that even scientific discovery requires assumptions (faith) and in order to move forward requires something greater than reason alone (intuition . . . another kind of seeing). This was the revolutionary turn.[9]

All of this reinforced discoveries like that of Werner Heisenberg. The world was much more complex than any Enlightenment thinker could have imagined, a lot messier, less rule-governed and more open-ended. It is closer to *chaordic* than merely orderly, and not nearly so predictable as we hoped. Caputo summarizes:

> The hermeneutical turn, the linguistic turn, and the revolutionary turn taken in a Kuhnian analysis of science—that is to say, the collective idea that human thinking turns on the ability to move among shifting perspectives, vocabularies and paradigms, none of which has dropped from the sky—make up what we will call the postmodern turn.[10]

Plumb, a postmodern singer/songwriter, puts it like this:

> Every point of view has another angle
> And every angle has its merit
> But it all comes down to faith
> That's the way I see it . . .
>
> There's a God-shaped hole in all of us
> And the restless soul is searching . . .[11]

See also "Kuhn, Thomas," "Epistemology," and "Postmodern"

---

9. Ibid., 48.
10. Ibid., 49.
11. Plumb, "God Shaped Hole."

Hospitality

When *Missional Church* was published in 1998 it redefined the conversation around the gospel and culture. At that time Inagrace Dietterich wrote,

> We too often forget the radical nature of Jesus' life and work. Religious leaders challenged him not because of his doctrine but because of those to whom he extended God's gracious and loving hospitality.
>
> Contemporary images of community or hospitality tend to exhibit what Parker Palmer calls an "ideology of intimacy." They emphasize sameness, closeness, warmth and comfort. Difference, distance, conflict and sacrifice are alien to this approach and therefore are to be avoided at all costs.
>
> Missional communities, shaped by faith in Jesus Christ and the gifts and fruit of the Holy Spirit, present a different image ... In a world increasingly "full of strangers, estranged from their own past, culture, and country, from their neighbors, friends and family, from their deepest self and their God," missional communities ... evidence ... the welcoming news of the reign of God.[12]

Henri Nouwen says that hospitality is not the heart of the gospel—hospitality *is* the gospel. He comments on John 15—Make your home in me as I make mine in you—that Jesus offers us an intimate place that we can call home. "Home is that place or space where we do not have to be afraid but can let go of our defenses and be free, free from worries, free from tensions, free from pressures. Home is where we can laugh and cry, embrace and dance ... Home is where we can rest and be healed ... a good place to be, it is the house of love."[13] There are two houses in this world: the house of fear, and the house of love. When the anxious questions of the world become our preoccupation, we are living in the house of fear. But Jesus offers us an alternative and invites us to live in his house, the house of love. It is only when we live from this place of rest and acceptance that we can offer a free space to others.

Elsewhere, Nouwen reflects that we cannot offer this safe and open space to others until we leave judgment behind. He writes, "To die to our neighbors is to stop judging them, to stop evaluating them, and thus

---

12. Deiterich, "Missional Church," 179.
13. Nouwen, *Lifesigns*, 8–9.

become compassionate. Compassion can never co-exist with judgment because judgment creates the distance, the distinction, which prevents us from really being with the other."[14]

Nouwen describes three movements that involve three sets of polarities in our process of formation.[15] The first movement is toward our inner self. In this movement we vacillate between the poles of loneliness and solitude. The second movement is toward our fellow humans. In this movement we vacillate between hostility and hospitality. The third movement is toward God. In this movement we vacillate between illusion and prayer.

Nouwen begins with the universal experience of loneliness. We are all essentially alone. In the midst of a crowd, or in our most intimate moments of sharing, we retain a sense of separation from others. Unless we are well and deeply loved, this sense of isolation can become unbearable. Nouwen argues that by courageously embracing the reality of our individual isolation, we can discover a hidden beauty. He suggests that we must transform our aloneness into a fruitful solitude, which is the beginning of the spiritual life.[16]

The second movement is from hostility to hospitality, and transforms fear, born in loneliness, into a welcoming and reconciling space.[17] Our goal is to "convert the *hostis* into a *hospes*, the enemy into a guest."[18] When we live in fear, we live in a small, enclosed world. We build strong walls to avoid the encounter with others and their pain. This second movement requires a rejection of ambivalence or distrust towards strangers and the commitment to produce an environment (a free and friendly space) where a stranger may begin to convert their own loneliness into solitude. "Hospitality is not to change people, but to offer them the space where change may take place."[19]

Last fall I received a book titled, *Living Gently in a Violent World*. In the introduction the author tells this story:

---

14. Nouwen, *The Way of the Heart*, 36.
15. Nouwen, *Reaching Out*.
16. Ibid., 39.
17. Ibid., 65.
18. Ibid., 66.
19. Ibid., 51.

Hospitality

> A few years ago I was teaching a course on pastoral care. It was a distance-learning course [and among] the students was one who had no sight and another who was profoundly deaf and spoke through an interpreter. At one point in the class, people where sharing their various spiritual experiences. The woman who was deaf, Angela, began to tell us about a dream she'd had. In that dream she has met with Jesus in heaven. She and Jesus talked for some time, and she said she had never experienced such peace and joy. "Jesus was everything I had hoped he would be," she said. And his signing was amazing![20]

For Angela heaven's perfection did not involve physical healing, but acceptance. It was a place where relational and communication barriers that exist for her were finally removed. What had led to exclusion and anxiety no longer mattered.

Hospitality features in virtually all of the missional orders within the new monastic movement (see *New Monasticism* below).[21] In the Northumbria rule, for example, it is framed within the call to be available and vulnerable: "firstly to be available to God in the *cell* of our own heart when we can be turned towards Him, and seek His face; then to be available to others in a call to exercise *hospitality*, recognizing that in welcoming others we honor and welcome the Christ Himself."[22]

Within the broader emerging conversation, the ongoing concern for the other is manifest in a new openness to particularity and difference, and a fresh awareness that the modern divisions of sacred and secular are often artificial and misleading. LeRon Shults closes his essay like this: "Yes, churches are called to become holy, but this does not require isolationist walls that protect 'our' sacrality from 'their' supposed profanity. Missional care in the way of Christ is embedded in the concrete, mundane concerns of oppressed others."[23] These are hopeful signs that the church is moving toward a wider ecumenism in the spirit of Christ.

See also "Nouwen, Henri" and "Formation, Spiritual"

---

20. Hauerwas and Swinton, *Living Gently in a Violent World*, 8.

21. Hospitality was also a major concern of Jacques Derrida. He asked, "Is not hospitality an interruption of the self"? For Derrida the responsibility toward the other was toward their individuality and singularity. See for example Westmoreland, "Interruptions: Derrida and Hospitality."

22. Northumbria Community.

23 Shults, "Reforming Ecclesiology in Emerging Churches."

I

Imago and Incarnation(al)

Imago

It is impossible to talk about the *missio Dei* without speaking about two other things: the *imago*, and culture. James K. A. Smith writes,

> The "image of God" (*imago Dei*) is not some de facto property of *Homo Sapiens* (whether will or reason or language or what have you); rather, the image of God is a task, a mission. As Richard Middleton comments, "The *imago Dei* designates the royal office or calling of human beings as God's representatives and agents in the world, granted authorized power to share in God's rule or administration of the earth's resources and creatures."[1]

We are commissioned as God's image bearers with the task of ruling and caring for creation. This cultural mandate includes the task of cultivating it, seeing and then working with its latent potentials through human making—in short, through creating culture. Smith quotes Middleton again: "Imaging God thus involves representing and perhaps extending in some way God's rule on earth through ordinary communal practices of human sociocultural life."[2]

In Genesis God sets humanity in creation as his image bearer, evoking the images of a priestly ambassador of the creation. In the ancient Near East there were two fixed components of religious life: temple and priest. Middleton writes that, "just as no pagan temple in the ancient Near East could be complete without the installation of the cult image of the deity, so creation in Genesis 1 is not complete (or 'very good') until God creates humanity on the sixth day as *imago Dei*, in order to represent and mediate the divine presence on earth."[3] *But the temple has not appeared yet.*

---

1. Smith, *Desiring the Kingdom*, 163.
2. Middleton, *The Liberating Image*, 60.
3. Ibid., 87.

Incarnation(al)

It is creation itself that is the sanctuary, and humanity is commissioned to priestly service in the sanctuary of the creation itself. That we increasingly narrowed this task to religious service in a building only points to our tendency to shrink God to our size, to localize and tame God so that we are can meet Him on our terms.

To rediscover the wild and dangerous God is to then rediscover our vocation. As our understanding of God expands, so our understanding of our selves grows and expands, and our understanding of the purposes of God in creation and redemption expand. As we move on to talk about the meaning of the incarnation, we'll build on this perspective.

See also "God"

INCARNATION(AL)

But to apprehend
The point of intersection of the timeless
With time, is an occupation for the saint.[4]

The third chapter of *The Shaping of Things to Come* is titled "Incarnational Ecclesiology." Essentially this is an ecclesiology of mission, founded on the reality and mode of Jesus arrival among us, a mode beautifully captured in *The Message*: the word became flesh and entered the neighborhood. No comfortable, objective distancing there!

Frost and Hirsch argue that the missional church is *incarnational*, as opposed to *attractional*. It "disassembles itself and seeps into the cracks and crevices of a society in order to be Christ to those who don't yet know him."[5]

Some of the theological implications are carefully outlined in *Shaping* as identification, locality, beyond-in-the-midst, and the human image of God. One of the keys is that "the Incarnation provides us with the missional means by which the gospel can become a genuine part of a people group without damaging the cultural frameworks that provide a

---

4. T. S. Eliot, *Four Quartets*.
5. Frost and Hirsch, *The Shaping of Things to Come*, 12.

Incarnation(al)

sense of history and meaning."[6] They rightly note that accommodation is a risk,[7] but our practice in modernity was the opposite extreme: cultural imperialism.

They further conclude that "incarnational mission implies a real and abiding presence among a group of people," and that "incarnational mission implies a sending impulse rather than an extractional one." To Frost and Hirsch incarnational mission means that, "people will get to experience Jesus on the inside of their culture's meaning systems."[8] By this they point out that we have tamed God and dressed Jesus as a middle-class WASP, much like Ned in *The Simpsons*. We need to experience the Jesus of the gospels in the places we live. The challenge of the incarnational church is to be read by the gospel.

Moreover, "outreach" is not enough when it defaults to "in-drag." The gaze of the church must turn outward to the neighborhoods where it is placed. One helpful analogy is that of "wells versus fences."[9] In the American west, ranchers often use fences to control cattle. In the wild Australian outback, where the spaces are too large, ranchers locate cattle by digging wells. They are less concerned about locating who is in or out than that all are drawn to a common center.

Incarnation strongly implies a theology of place. Simon Carey Holt writes, "the Incarnation is about much more than God revealed in human experience, but God revealed and encountered in place—and in the most domestic of places one can imagine."[10] Eugene Peterson writes,

> Everything that the Creator God does in forming us humans is done in place. It follows from this that since we are his creatures and can hardly escape the conditions of our making, for us everything that has to do with God is also in place. All living is local: this land, this neighborhood, these trees and streets and houses, this work, these people.[11]

It would be wrong to talk about the incarnation without talking about the world of particulars. Modernity privileged the Universal, and

---

6. Ibid., 37.
7. Thus the name of one of Frost's articles, "Evangelism as Risky Negotiation."
8. Ibid., 40.
9. Ibid., 47.
10. Holt, *God Next Door*, 63.
11. Peterson, *Christ Plays in Ten Thousand Places*, 72.

Incarnation(al)

in postmodernity we privilege local narratives, and the ordinary things of daily life. As Carrie Newcomer put it,

> Holy is the dish and drain
> The soap and sink, the cup and plate
> And the warm wool socks, and the cold white tile
> Showerheads and good dry towels
> And frying eggs sound like psalms
> With a bit of salt measured in my palm
> It's all a part of a sacrament
> As holy as a day is spent . . .[12]

See also "God," "Formation, Spiritual," and "Missional"

---

12. Newcomer, *The Gathering of Spirits*, 1. Permission for use granted by Carrie Newcomer, 2002. All rights reserved. From the album *The Gathering of Spirits*.

J

Justice

> Thy kingdom come,
> Thy will be done
> On earth as it is in heaven ...[1]

In the early 1900s, the gospel became divided between a spiritual, eternal destiny issue and a social transformation issue. Pietism or activism seemed to generally be the options, though groups like the Salvation Army managed to adhere to one gospel longer than most. But for many believers, justice became something to expect in the next life, and something divorced from the reality of God's reign in this world. Dallas Willard represents this dualistic perspective as the gospel of sin management. Willard comments that, "the Gospel isn't a one-time event, it's a daily participation with Christ in the Kingdom life."[2]

The Cross is more than atonement, it is identification. It is also more than an ending, it inaugurates a new kingdom and a new community under a different Lord.[3] Newbigin writes that, "It is surely a fact of inexhaustible significance that what our Lord left behind Him was not a book, nor a creed, nor a system of thought, nor a rule of life, but a visible community. He committed the entire work of salvation to that community."[4] There is

---

1. Matt. 6:9–10.
2. Willard, "Stepping Into Community," 3.
3. Thus John Driver comments, "The church is by definition a community. The question which confronts the church today therefore is, 'What kind of community will we be?'" In *Community and Commitment*, 21.
4. Op Cit., *Household of God*.

no dualism in the gospel, such that salvation makes us nice people but doesn't affect the way we live with one another. Salvation is made visible—is an expression of shalom—when God reconciles us one to another.

The Old Testament prophets continually thundered at the people that God's justice was to be seen and expressed in the way they lived toward one another, and toward the stranger. In the Old Testament Israel was to represent the character of God in their relationships—shalom means more than peace, but also health and harmony. In the New Testament this mandate remains as life under the reign of Christ in his just kingdom. Justice is not merely an ethic, then, but a manifestation of the eschatological reign of God.

Stanley Hauerwas and William Willimon write, "In saying 'the church doesn't have a social strategy, the church *is* a social strategy,' we are attempting to indicate an alternative way of looking at the political, social significance of the church."[5]

> Rejecting both the individualism of the conversionists and the secularism of the activists ... the confessing church finds it main political task to lie, not in the personal transformation of individual hearts or the modification of society, but rather in the congregation's determination to worship Christ in all things. The confessing church, like the conversionist church, also calls people to conversion, but it depicts that conversion as a long process of being baptismally engrafted into a new people, an alternative *polis*, a countercultural social structure called church. It seeks to influence the world by being the church, that is, by being something the world is not and can never be ... The confessing church seeks the visible church, a place, clearly visible to the world, in which people are faithful to their promises, love their enemies, tell the truth, honor the poor, suffer for righteousness, and thereby testify to the amazing community-creating power of God ...[6]

See also "Empire" and "Incarnation"

---

5. Hauerwas and Willimon, *Resident Aliens*, 45.
6. Ibid.

Kingdom, and Kuhn

Kingdom

> The "political" metaphor, "Kingdom," insists on a gospel that includes everything and everyone under the rule of God. God is no religious glow to warm a dark night. Christ is no esoteric truth with which to form a Gnostic elite. The Christian faith is an out-in-the-open, strenuous, legislating, conquering totality: God is sovereign, nothing and no one is exempt from his rule.[1]

I was reading this morning in the gospel of Isaiah, chapter thirty-two. I was minding my own business when a picture of the reign of God burst off the page. The chapter opens like this: Behold—a king will reign in righteousness.

That's a great opening for the story. In the verses following the prophet paints a picture of what justice looks like, and there are some warnings against complacency. Then in verse 15 we discover how this transformation from the city of man to the city of God takes place. The palaces are forsaken, the city deserted . . .

> Until the Spirit is poured upon us from on high,
> And the wilderness becomes a fruitful field,
> And the fruitful field is counted as a forest.
> Then justice will dwell in the wilderness,
> And righteousness remain in the fruitful field.
> The work of righteousness will be shalom,
> And the effect of righteousness, quietness and assurance forever.

---

1. Peterson, *Reversed Thunder*, 3.

Kingdom

> My people will dwell in a peaceful habitation,
> In secure dwellings, and in quiet resting places ...

I love this. The picture of the coming of the Spirit is not shaking and baking—not even prophesying—but is a picture of a transformed world.

When God's kingdom comes, His shalom, everything changes. Brian McLaren writes,

> The Kingdom of God ... is a revolutionary, counter-cultural movement-proclaiming a ceaseless rebellion against the tyrannical trinity of money, sex, and power. Its citizens resist the occupation of this invisible Caesar through three categories of spiritual practice. First ... generosity ... second ... prayer ... finally ... fasting.[2]

Where is the kingdom of God now in the midst of the kingdoms of this world? This question is complex, yet it shapes our mission. Howard Snyder calls the church to recognize the mystery of the kingdom, pointing to Jesus' teaching in the parables.[3] Snyder identifies the paradox of the kingdom—it is both present and future, embodied in the individual and in the community, and is both distinct from and identical to the church.[4]

While we are forced to embrace paradox, other affirmations are simpler. The nature of the kingdom of God is tied directly to the *missio Dei*. If the mission of God is to redeem, reconcile, and restore creation to its original purpose through the covenant community, then the kingdom of God is manifest wherever this restoration is being realized. Wright expresses it like this:

> Because Jesus is raised from the dead, God's new world has begun. We are not only the beneficiaries of new creation, we are the agents of it when we do new creation. So when we encourage one another in the church to be active in projects of new creation—of healing, of hope for communities—we are standing on the ground that Jesus has won in his resurrection. God intends to renew the world and what we do in the present matters.[5]

---

2. McLaren, *The Secret Message of Jesus*, 134.
3. Snyder, *Models of the Kingdom*.
4. Ibid. For each of these points of tension or polarities, Snyder provides New Testament references: present/future (Mark 1:15; Matt. 6:10), individual/communal (Matt. 13:44; Luke 12:32), spirit/matter (1 Cor. 15:50; Luke 4:18–21), gradual/climactic (Mark 4:26–28; Matt. 25:1–6), divine/human (Luke 19:11–27; Matt. 6:33), and church as same/different (Matt. 16:19; Matt. 7:21).
5. Lowery, "N. T. Wright on Resurrection," par. 1.

God's kingdom opens a rule of justice and peace. When Jesus announces his ministry by proclaiming the arrival of the kingdom he is appealing to the grand story of God's mighty acts in history and declaring that it is reaching its climax. Heaven is arriving on earth. Wright continues,

> I put it this way for my audiences: "there is life after life after death." A person goes to heaven first and then to the new heavens and new earth. The New Testament doesn't have much to say about what happens to people immediately after they die. It's much more interested in the anticipation of the ultimate new world within this one.[6]

See also "Empire," "Exile," "Gospel," and "Missional"

KUHN, THOMAS

It was Thomas Kuhn who coined the phrase *paradigm shift*. Kuhn tracked several of the greatest breakthroughs the twentieth century, and discovered that great breakthroughs do not occur based strictly on factual evidence. Instead there are two different phases of scientific progress. In the first phase, scientists work within a *paradigm* (a set of accepted beliefs that are a framework and a lens for their study). When the foundation of the paradigm weakens and new theories and scientific methods begin to replace it, the next phase of scientific discovery occurs. Kuhn argues that progress from one paradigm to another has no logical method, but instead is based on intuitive and supra-rational factors. Kuhn coined the phrase paradigm shift to describe this process, and his arguments have occasioned a great deal of controversy.

Then in 1966, Michael Polanyi, a philosopher of science, advocated a new theory of knowledge based on personal and tacit knowledge. He questioned not only the possibility but the wisdom of advocating objective knowledge.

> The declared aim of modern science is to establish a strictly detached, objective knowledge. Any falling short of this ideal is accepted only as a temporary imperfection, which we must aim at

6. Ibid., 1.

eliminating. But suppose that tacit thought forms an indispensable part of all knowledge, then the ideal of eliminating all personal elements of knowledge would, in effect, aim at the destruction of all knowledge. The idea of exact science would be fundamentally misleading and possibly a source of devastating fallacies.[7]

Polanyi and Kuhn hunted the same game, their target the supra-rational dimension of knowledge, evident in most scientific discovery but rarely admitted. To openly acknowledge the tacit dimension meant an admission that science was not founded on pure and objective knowledge alone. In the minds of some, this was to invite criticism and chaos, to open Pandora's box, to begin an uncertain process that would erode the foundation of modern science.

Perhaps more to the point, the admission that scientific discovery was not founded after all on pure reason and objectivity meant dethroning the scientist himself from his lofty priesthood.

See also "Epistemology," "Gregory, Saint," and "Heisenberg"

---

7. Polanyi, *The Tacit Dimension*, 20.

L

L'avenir, Laity, Leadership, and Liminal

L'AVENIR

> Is it possible to live in the humility of knowing that our purpose, as clearly as we self-define it, is but "a husk of meaning"? The task is really to become superb listeners. Heidegger wrote that waiting, listening, was the most profound way to serve God.[1]

One of the most fundamental precursors of emergence is emptiness, and an ability to embrace mystery. On the other hand, one of the most fundamental characteristics of modernity is the search for certainty. No wonder we haven't been very good at waiting!

Yet our faith is rooted in a fundamental mystery. And the heroes of faith, described by the writer of Hebrews, seemed comfortable with a fundamental insecurity: They went out, not knowing where they were going. Faith is a trusting in something beyond sight, something we have not yet seen, with an inner confidence . . . *con-fides* . . . a deep faith in someone who cares for us.

The goal of the gospel is a living community, built around a common knowledge of and intimacy with Christ. There are no professionals, only amateurs: *amati* is Latin for lover and professionals are hirelings who arrive with the baggage of identity and status. Those who arrive with so much to protect rarely have the courage to lose sight of the shore; but those who arrive as lovers—ah!—these ones will give all that they have simply to behold His face.

---

1. Wheatley, "Consumed by Either Fire or Fire," 4.

L'avenir

In one Jesus movie there is a scene near the end where Jesus appears to His disciples in the upper room. Together they kneel in love and awe as He smiles at them. They are united in worship and in love. There are no apostles or leaders ... together they are lovers and servants, and in His presence they are all on the same level.

Community and mission are both about love and emptiness of our own agendas. Only those who forsake all for the sake of love can reach a city not built with hands. So often we think of science as quantitatively a different pursuit than the world of faith. We reason that faith is about uncertainty and science about certainty. Faith is playful; science is serious.

Jacques Derrida writes on l'avenir; *to come*. Derrida, considered agnostic by most commentators, often evidences a profound faith in a God he refuses to name. He recognizes that to name what we don't know is only another means of reaching for control; he stands and waits.

> In general, I try to distinguish between what one calls the future and "l'avenir." The future is that which—tomorrow, later, next century—will be. There's a future which is predictable, programmed, scheduled, foreseeable. But there is a future, *l'avenir* (to come) which refers to someone who comes whose arrival is totally unexpected. For me, that is the real future. That which is totally unpredictable. The other who comes without my being able to anticipate their arrival. So if there is a real future beyond this other known future, it's *l'avenir* in that it's the coming of the other when I am completely unable to foresee their arrival.[2]

I know that many of us read this quote and are puzzled. Isn't part of finding Christ ... or being found by him ... a secure knowing of who we are? That is ... before we were lost and now we are found. Haven't we then somehow arrived?

Well yes and no.

Here in my fifty-second year, I seem so much more sure of a few things, but much less certain about so much else. I am still discovering that the Jesus I thought I knew is a cultural icon, very unlike the Jesus of the gospels. The more I discover about the Jesus I expected, the more I feel like the Jews in the first century: confused, doubtful. The more I read the gospels, the more Jesus of Nazareth is unlike the God proclaimed in most churches. The closer I come to the light, the dimmer seems my reason.

---

2. Kronick, *Derrida and the Future of Literature*, 69.

L'avenir

But maybe there is hope in acknowledging that God is truly "other." There is a real future beyond this known future, and it requires humility, emptiness, and surrender. The future we expected—the Jesus we thought we knew—will never appear on this earth because he was largely a construct of the God we thought we needed. But if we admit our foolishness, perhaps we can open space where our blindness can become sight.

Last year a friend related to me that the physicists who are researching quantum dynamics and who are working with the very smallest particles came up against another mystery. It seems that while there were some things that were definable, one of the largest questions remaining was about the power in matter. No one knows where it comes from. This caused one scientist to theorize that perhaps the power is in the blank spaces.

Blank spaces are what we lose when we organize. Blank spaces are those elements of shred life that remain shrouded in mystery. In fact, community itself *is* a mystery. You can plan it, organize it, pray for it, and still not get it. It requires something spontaneous and unreachable by human effort and thought alone. It requires more weakness than strength, and we aren't very good at weakness. Community is a gift, and we aren't good at receiving. Even those of us with faith have lost perspective. Eugene Peterson writes,

> The secularized mind is terrorized by mysteries. Thus it makes lists, labels people, assigns roles, and solves problems. But a solved life is a reduced life. These tightly buttoned-up people never take great faith risks or make convincing love talk. They deny or ignore the mysteries and diminish human existence to what can be managed, controlled, and fixed. We live in a cult of experts who explain and solve . . .
>
> But "there are things," wrote Marianne Moore, "that are important beyond all this fiddle." The old time guide of souls asserts the priority of the "beyond" over "this fiddle." Who is available for this kind of work other than pastors? A few poets, maybe; and children, always. But children are not good guides, and most of the poets have lost interest in God. That leaves pastors as guides through the mysteries.[3]

See also "Heisenberg" and "Mystery."

---

3. Peterson, *The Contemplative Pastor*, 65.

Laity

While this dictionary has an entry for laity, it has none for clergy. It could be that I am showing a profound bias!

But while we are all *laos*, by biblical definition—we are all priests and princes and prophets—we are not all clergy, at least not in the cultural sense in which we use this word. The ordained and professional class of Christian minister is a recent development, and many perceptive leaders say it is neither biblical nor healthy. Alan Roxburgh, for one, claims that the professional model, with its focus on one dominant, usually shepherd-type leader, is "killing pastors," leading to "terrible discouragement and loneliness, and creating a deep sense of personal failure."[4] As a result of this prevailing leadership arrangement, many pastors lack a day-to-day interface with peer leaders who share some things in common, but who are otherwise very different from them in perspective, giftedness and experience. Lead pastors are often expected to embody numerous roles and capacities, often regarded as the lone, anointed point leaders who are supposed to develop all the other leaders. Eddie Gibbs notes, "Our training models are conditioned by a Christendom mindset and the agendas of the academy. As a consequence, we neglect the three other areas of ministry listed first in Ephesians 4, all of which are of critical importance in the missional church: the gifts of apostle, prophet and evangelist."[5]

But there are other reasons why we tend to view Jesus followers in two classes. Our understanding of the gospel itself has been secularized and narrowed.

> One reason why the churches have not helped the laity to see the Christian significance of their vocation in the world is that the churches had lost sight of the cosmic dimension of the gospel. This could only lead to self-centered ecclesiasticism or pietism. When we realize again that Christ is the hope of the world, we see also that activity in the world is meaningful. It does not carry its meaning within itself, but it has a goal, an end: the kingdom.
>
> Christians are men and women who live toward that future and manifest this faith by acts which express their hope and expectation. At a time when—because of the collapse of the doctrine of progress—there is a great danger that all human effort is poisoned

---

4. Roxburgh and Romanuk, *The Missional Leader*, 190.
5. Ibid., xiii.

by a sense of futility, the Church has the great opportunity of re-creating a sense of the meaningfulness and worthiness of worldly vocation.[6]

The value of worldly vocation is strongly linked to a biblical anthropology. What we make of the image of God connects to our understanding of priesthood. In the last century that understanding increasingly narrowed to an in-ecclesia vocation, and away from a cultural mandate. Apart from the recovery of a much broader sense of priesthood—one that will be framed within the larger *missio Dei*—we are unlikely to move beyond the dualism of Christian classes. James Smith writes:

> The "image of God" (*imago Dei*) is not some *de facto* property of *Homo Sapiens* (whether will or reason or language or what have you); rather, the image of God is a task, a mission. As Richard Middleton comments, "The *imago Dei* designates the royal office or calling of human beings as God's representatives and agents in the world, granted authorized power to share in God's rule or administration of the earth's resources and creatures." We are commissioned as God's image bearers, his vice-regents, charged with the task of "ruling" and caring for creation, which includes the task of cultivating it, unfolding and unfurling its latent possibilities through human making—in short, through *culture*. Imaging God thus involves representing and perhaps extending in some way God's rule on earth through ordinary communal practices of human sociocultural life.[7]

See also "Imago Dei"

Leadership

> Leaders should not seek power or status;
> people will not then crave power or status.
> If scarce goods are not valued highly,
> people will have no need to steal them.
> If there is nothing available to arouse passion,
> people will remain content and satisfied.

---

6. Visser't Hooft, as cited in Hall, *The Stewardship of Life in the Kingdom of Death*, i.
7. Op Cit., 163.

Leadership

> The truly wise do lead
> by instilling humility and open-mindedness,
> by providing for fair livelihoods,
> by discouraging personal ambition,
> by strengthening the bone-structure of the people.
>
> The wise avoid evil and radical reform;
> thus the foolish do not obstruct them.
> They work serenely, with inner quiet.
>
> The best leaders, the people do not notice.
> The next best, the people honor and praise.
> The next, the people fear;
> and the next, the people hate.
>
> If you have no faith, people will have no faith
> in you, and you must resort to oaths.
>
> When the best leader's work is done
> the people say: "We did it ourselves!"[8]

Lao Tzu and his culture are many centuries distant in time and social geography. But it could be that our western culture has drifted so far from its roots in the east that words from the east that can help us recall a biblical perspective. Roxburgh and Romanuk describe the role of leadership in our time: "to cultivate environments wherein the Spirit of God may call forth and unleash the missional imagination of the people of God."[9] This is one promise of a leadership community, connecting to our need to re-imagine ourselves as missionaries in the post-Christendom culture we live in.

The question of leadership has dominated ecclesial imagination for the past twenty years. The result has not been renewal and the church in the west remains in decline, founded on models of religious consumerism and with more evidence of leadership cults than a leadership culture. Postmodernists reject authority in position in favor of authority in relationship. They do not buy into hierarchies, and they tend to assign authority only when it is earned. They don't respect leaders who are "over" but not "among." This aligns with the New Testament teaching on the priesthood of believers and Jesus teaching that the greatest among you must be the servant of all.

8. Heider, *The Tao of Leadership*, 17.
9. Op Cit., 75.

> In the deepest sense, distinction between leaders and followers is meaningless. In every moment of life, we are simultaneously leading and following. There is never a time when our knowledge, judgment and wisdom are not more useful and applicable than that of another. There is never a time when the knowledge, judgment and wisdom of another are not more useful and applicable than ours. At any time that "other" may be superior, subordinate, or peer.[10]

The leadership style that once dominated our culture and our churches is becoming passé. Instead of the Lone Ranger, we have Frodo: the Clint Eastwoods and Sylvester Stallones are replaced by ordinary men. Frodo, Aragorn and Neo (*The Matrix*) are self-questioning types who rely on those around them for strength, clarity, and purpose. Indeed, while they have a sense of the need for leadership and a willingness to sacrifice themselves, they may not even know the first step on the journey.

A critical element in framing leadership was recently identified in a simple statement by Stanley Hauerwas: "Leadership can't be abstracted from the communities that make it possible."[11] Stan points to the soil—the living community itself, where all leadership begins. But we humans are meaning makers: we don't exist in undifferentiated soil, but constantly reflect on the meaning of the places we dwell. There have been two popular lenses for ecclesia: the church as an organism and the church as an institution. As far back as *Community of the King,* Howard Snyder was making this distinction, but it existed in the conversation of German theology long before as *Geselleschaft* and *Gemeinschaft*. Snyder explored the distinction more thoroughly in 1983, arguing that our dominant metaphors—the language we use—have power. Whether we choose a mechanistic image or an organic image influences the kind of community we are. He wrote that, "as man and woman become like their gods, so they become like their models. A machine model (a technosystem) produces human robots; an organic model (an ecosystem) produces healthy persons."[12]

See also "Google."

---

10. Hock, *The Art of Chaordic Leadership*, 1.
11. Hauerwas, "What Only the Church Can Do," par. 1.
12. Snyder, *Liberating the Church*.

LIMINAL

In *Pacing the Cage,* Bruce Cockburn sings that, "Sometimes the best map will not guide you/You can't see what's round the bend."

One April Sunday my family and I visited a young church community in our town. On the way to the meeting we noticed two very different restaurant signs. The first invited, "Come in from the cold; warm food and hot drinks." The second proclaimed, "Swing into spring. Escape the heat with our smoothies and frappacinos."

Contradiction is one of the elements of *liminality*. Is it winter, or spring? When the seasons are in transition, and the old season hasn't quite given way to the new, we don't know quite what kind of weather to expect or even how to dress on a given morning. When we walk out the door it might be hot, or it might be cold. Worse, it may start out warm then shift to cold while we are on the road. We are plunged into uncertainty. When the church is in transition, the same kind of confusion surfaces. Even casual conversations can become complex, with people using language in very different ways. Words like church and evangelism and even Christian carry baggage they didn't once possess. We struggle for definition, even reacting against it. Moving from a Baptist gathering to an E Free gathering becomes an experience in cultural shift, even within the same town.

Liminality is a place in between. It is emptiness and nowhere. Adolescence is the liminal space between childhood and adulthood. But liminality is more than a point along the way to somewhere else. It represents anti-structure to structure, chaos to order. The place between two world views is a liminal place. It is a place of dying and rebirth, even of metamorphosis, the place where the caterpillar spins its cocoon and disappears from view. Liminality is Israel in the desert, Jesus in the tomb.

The Latin word *limina* means threshold. Liminality is where all transformation happens. It is when we are betwixt and between, and therefore by definition not in control. Nothing new happens as long as we are inside our self-constructed comfort zone. Much of our day-to-day effort at life is toward maintaining our personal little world. Richard Rohr comments that,

> . . . much of the work of God is to get people into liminal space, and to keep them there long enough so they can learn something essential. It is the ultimate teachable space . . . maybe the only one. Most spiritual giants try to live lives of "chronic liminality" in

some sense. They know it is the only position that insures ongoing wisdom, broader perspective and ever-deeper compassion. The Jewish prophets . . . St. Francis, Gandhi, and John the Baptist come to mind.[13]

Liminal space tends to be counterintuitive. In liminal space we need to walk in the opposite direction. We not eat instead of eat—we remain silent instead of talking. We search for emptiness instead of fullness. In liminal space we descend and intentionally do not ascend; "status reversal" instead of status-seeking. We indulge in shadow boxing instead of ego confirmation.

Few of us choose liminal space. Instead, God usually has to engineer the journey. Someone we trusted fails us; a job we counted on suddenly ends; a child or spouse dies; we are struck blind on the road to Emmaus. Once we arrive there, we are disinclined to call it home. This is why spiritual directors and counselors are often sought in times of transition . . . we need outward support and encouragement to endure liminal space. On our own we tend to run for security, back to the familiar gardens of Egypt.

See also "Communitas" and "L'Avenir"

---

13. Rohr, *"Days Without Answers in a Narrow Space,"* 1.

Merton, Memory, Missional, and Mystery

Merton, Thomas

> Thomas Merton told a fellow monk, "If I make anything out of the fact that I am Thomas Merton, I am dead. And if you make anything out of the fact that you are in charge of the pig barn, you are dead." Merton's solution? "Quit keeping score altogether and surrender yourself with all your sinfulness to God who sees neither the score nor the scorekeeper but only his child redeemed by Christ."[1]

I've read only a handful of books by Merton, and only two about him, but the influence of these on my own life has been substantial. I include him here not for that personal influence, but because his name continues to pop up among my friends, and in those I read. Why is this?

It may be because Merton was a saint, but it seems to me it is equally because he was a poet and a writer. That intrigues me, because it embodies a certain paradox. A trappist monk, supposed to embrace solitude and silence, is well known because his life was poured out in words. Some years ago Vinson Synan, Dean of the Regent University School of Divinity, remarked: "No movement lasts very long unless it is buttressed by good thought and strong theology," Synan said. "Experience is important, but it's what you write down that affects future generations."[2]

And write and reflect is what Merton did, and loved to do. An MA in English literature, the real battle for his soul may have been fought

---

1. Sussman and Sussman, *Thomas Merton*, 94.
2. Synan, *Charisma*, 24.

between those two worlds. In the end, he held them both together. Not long before his death he wrote,

> There is a need for effort, deepening, change and transformation. Not that I must undertake a special project of self-transformation or that I must "work on myself." In that regard, it would be better to forget it. Just go for walks, live in peace, let change come quietly and invisibly on the inside. But I do have a past to break with, and accumulation of inertia, waste, wrong, foolishness, rot, junk, a great need of clarification, of mindfulness . . . a return to genuine practice, right effort . . . need for the Spirit.
>
> Hang on to the clear light![3]

Merton was heavily influenced by some great literary figures, probably the best known of which is Gerard Manley Hopkins. Merton loved the poetry of Hopkins and wrote his Master's thesis on Hopkins' work. In Hopkins he found a concept borrowed from Duns Scotus, similar to inner landscape—*thingicity*, or *thingness*: Inscape is the inner texture of a thing that is derived uniquely from God the endlessly inventive Creator. Inscape plays a major role in Hopkins thought and in his poetry.

> GLORY be to God for dappled things—
> For skies of couple-colour as a brinded cow;
> For rose-moles all in stipple upon trout that swim;
> Fresh-firecoal chestnut-falls; finches' wings;
> Landscape plotted and pieced—fold, fallow, and plough;
> And áll trádes, their gear and tackle and trim.[4]

Merton equates the unique thingness of a thing, its inscape, to sanctity. Holiness itself is grounded in God's creation. To the extent that a created thing honors God's unique idea of it, it is holy. Holiness thus connects to vocation (from the Latin *vocare* for voice) in two ways. First, God creates through the word; He speaks and things *are*. Second, the things He creates respond to His present creative work, His moment by moment willing the world into existence through love, by becoming what they are. Creation may choose to remember its *thingness*, responding rightly to God's speech by expressing his unique word. We choose to become our true selves, or we copy something or someone else and become less than what we are. The more we choose our selves, the more we agree with the

---

3. Merton, *Woods, Shore, Desert*, 12.
4. Gardner, *Gerard Manley Hopkins*, "Pied Beauty," 30.

word God has spoken that is uniquely our self, the more we experience sanctity. Merton writes,

> No two created beings are exactly alike. And their individuality is no imperfection. On the contrary, the perfection of each created thing is not merely its conformity to an abstract type but in its own individual identity with itself.[5]

Thus it is in particularity that the love of God is most clearly expressed. God says, "I love this tree, this flower, this man" more than the idea of the thing. Later Merton writes,

> It is not humility to insist on being someone that you are not. It is as much as saying that you know better than God who you are and who you ought to be. How do you expect to arrive at the end of your own journey if you take the road to another man's city?[6]

See also "Formation, Spiritual" and "Imago"

Memory

> Faith begins, not in discovery, but in remembrance. The story began without us.[7]

We aren't very good at waiting. Transitions demand of us a security in something outside this earth. We lack the imagination to see God's newness, so we place our trust in progress, or maybe our own knowledge and abilities, and get discouraged, because our love has been love for the wrong thing. Yet we must believe, there is yet faith, even when our own weakness causes us to doubt, because the brokenness of Jesus became the path to the new world: "There's a crack in everything / that's how the light gets in."[8] The only good future is God's future, but it is a life born in death and a future rooted in the past. So memory becomes critical. We won't walk into God's good future if we have no memories of God's mighty acts on our behalf in the past. Or at least, we won't walk into the fullness

---

5. Merton, *New Seeds of Contemplation*, 29.
6. Ibid., 101.
7. Hauerwas and Willimon, *Resident Aliens*, 52.
8. Leonard Cohen, "Anthem."

of that future, with all the power and healing force for our communities that God intends. Again and again in Scripture, one of the fundamental rhythms is that of remembrance.

In our time we have lost our sense of identity, because we have lost our sense of place. We have lost our sense of place because we have lost our immersion in the ongoing story of God in history. Sometimes we lose that place because we are separated from deep community, the kind of caring, sharing, and mutual encouragement we all need. Fractured, fragmented, and distracted, we don't remember the stories of God and His people, or we have failed to make them our stories. But we can't know ourselves apart from those memories, or apart from the living body, because they are *our* memories, and *our* family.

In scripture we are constantly reminded of our identity as a *covenant people*. In times of exile we face the unique danger of loss of memory and loss of community. In that void, we are apt to believe the promises of the empire to give us a home, to bring us security, to provide meaning, and unlimited consumption in an eternal now. Who needs memory when life is so good today? Who needs community when we have everything we need?

God's people have faced other times like this. In Joshua 24, the generation who saw God's wonders in the desert have died off. The people have lost their sense of identity because they don't have those old memories. A renewal of covenant is necessary, and part of that renewal is the renewal of memory. What does Joshua do? He recounts the story of God's loving faithfulness, going back to Abraham. Then he calls the people to make a choice (24:15). Next he attempts to dissuade them: God is a holy God and a jealous God. Do they know what they are doing in the light of who God is? (24:19). In light of their determination, Joshua calls them to remove the idols from among them. He calls them to a heart commitment: a commitment of their entire being. Then he does two things which are quite interesting: He writes the words of their commitment in a book, and he sets up a large stone (24:26). He symbolizes the events of this covenant renewal for all to see, to establish a lasting memory.

Tell all his wonderful acts, is more than a simple refrain in David's song;[9] it is the fundamental work of the people (*liturgia*). Apart from memory we have no stories and without stories we have no identity.

---

9. 1 Chron. 16:9b.

Missional

Lacking identity we have no way to renew covenant, and no way to move forward as a people. And we must renew covenant, because we continually compromise and falter and fail.

> Only through the practice of memory will new possibility emerge. Without some form of memory, this sentence you are reading would make no sense... Without memory we become imprisoned in an absolute present, unaware of the direction we have come from, and therefore what direction we are heading in. Without memory there can be no momentum, no discernible passage of time, and therefore no movement or velocity.[10]

All these things come together in the New Testament at the Lord's Table. The story of Passover is brought into the present, and the memories of deliverance and the hope for a just future become one story. "This is the new covenant in my blood. Do this in memory of Me."

Remembrance unites past and present and we enter the lived story. In remembering God's mighty acts in history we incorporate the new tellers and hearers as part of the narrative. When we share the meal together it becomes *our* story. We become the new community as we take the new life into us. The shared meal is the center of our shared life as God's people because in sharing the meal we both proclaim and perform the gospel together. We become a sacrament and sign of the coming kingdom. And we are impelled into mission, because Jesus life was poured out for the world.

See also "Empire," "Exile," and "Kingdom"

Missional

Before the earth was created, the noun existed in the eternal counsels of God. But perhaps the verb also existed, in the great dance of love. And then out of that fullness came the earth and humankind, and the verb begat an adjective. And that, according to some versions, is when the trouble really started.

Around 1994 Australian theologian Charles Ringma stated,

---

10. Brueggemann, *Hopeful Imagination*, 56.

Missional

> The missional church vision is not a programmatic response to the crisis of relevance, purpose and identity that the church in the Western World is facing, but a recapturing of biblical views of the Church all too frequently abandoned, ignored, or obscured through long periods of church history. It is a renewed theological vision of the church in mission, which redefines the nature, the mission and the organization of the local church around Jesus' proclamation of the good news of the Kingdom. Missional Churches seek to respond to God's invitation to join Him in His mission in and for the world, as a sign, a servant and a foretaste of His Kingdom.[11]

Great stuff. Let's dig and prod a bit.

"NOT A PROGRAMMATIC RESPONSE"

In contrast to many visions of church renewal or church growth, we must move beyond pragmatism. Missional church is not a solution for declining attendance or reduced giving. It is not a new outreach program, or indeed any kind of program at all, but rather a rediscovery and re-appropriation of biblical views of the church that have long been obscured. One implication is that we have some work to do to de-clutter and unlearn before we begin building. Colin Greene writes, "To turn the missional language into a type of church identity is to miss altogether the Newbigin conviction that a missiological engagement with Western culture requires a break with Christendom presuppositions altogether and indeed, at heart, refers not to church identities but to a dynamic new form of public theology and praxis."[12]

"A RENEWED THEOLOGICAL VISION"

"Renewed," not a new discovery but a reaching back to something that was lost. Missional church is a renewed theological vision of the church in mission, and primarily a recovery of biblical identity around the good news of God's reign. As some scribe put it, (Bosch?) "it is not the Church of God that has a mission in the world, but the God of mission who has a Church in the world."[13] Our modern penchant to reduce the gospel to personal salvation or to the purpose of the church (as if mission were our possession) does an injustice to every theological category we

---

11. Transcript from a conference offered to me by Dr. Brown, 2009.
12. Greene, "Newbigin to Where?" 9.
13. Ascribed to David Bosch, source unknown.

Missional

know: Pneumatology, Christology, Soteriology, Missiology, Eschatology, Ecclesiology, Theology etc. The work of N. T. Wright and others in re-opening the discussion around the meaning of justification in the work of Paul and a re-appropriation of covenant language with reference to the gospel is helping us move beyond the narrative that has self at the center. Indeed, the challenge is an alternative social imaginary.[14]

"CHURCH . . . REDEFINED . . . AROUND JESUS PROCLAMATION"

While mission (*missio Dei*) precedes church (*ecclesia*), once the ball started rolling the movement is circular, interwoven like the double helix—church and mission. Church is community in mission, and mission produces shalom communities. But it is also critical to note that *missio Dei* means Trinity-in-mission. If we miss this piece we reinforce the cultural lens of individualism and then easily reinforce the privatist and dualist approach that is killing us. Here too covenant has a place.

"SIGN, SERVANT AND FORETASTE OF HIS KINGDOM"

Again, it is the kingdom that is primary. Jesus did not come preaching the church of God. But here too there is reciprocity, and church and kingdom are neither identical nor separable. Who paints this picture better than Newbigin, with the Trinitarian lens:

> The concern for mission is nothing less than this: the kingdom of God, the sovereign rule of the Father of Jesus over all humankind and over all creation. Mission . . . is the proclamation of the kingdom, the presence of the kingdom and the prevenience of the kingdom. By proclaiming the reign of God over all things the church acts out its faith that the Father of Jesus is indeed ruler of all. The church, by inviting all humankind to share in the mystery of the presence of the kingdom hidden in its life through its union with the crucified and risen life of Jesus, acts out the love of Jesus that took him to the cross. By obediently following where the Spirit leads, often in ways neither planned, known, nor understood, the church acts out the hope that it is given by the presence of the Spirit who is the living foretaste of the kingdom.[15]

See also "Kingdom," "Newbigin," and "Bosch"

---

14. See the explanation of Charles Taylor's concept further along under "S."
15. Newbigin, *The Open Secret*, 64.

Mystery

"Can't tell me there is no mystery" sings Cockburn.[16] And Bob Webber noted that the recovery of mystery is close to the heart of things in this postmodern space.

> It may broadly be said that the story of Christianity moves from mystery in the classical period, to institution in the medieval era, to individualism in the Reformation era, to reason in the modern era, and now, in the postmodern era, back to mystery.[17]

In a collection of essays written in 2004, Belden Lane reflects on the journey he had with his dying father. He relates a story from the life of Gerard Manley Hopkins. Hopkins was on the path to a remote monastery when he was distracted from his self-conscious quest for spiritual attainment by the raw beauty of the play of light on stone. I have no choice, he protested, but to be alive to this landscape and this light. Because of his delay, he never got to the monastery. Lane writes,

> Compelling his imagination the most was that the awesome beauty of this fierce land was in no way conditioned by his frail presence. It was not there for him. The stream would continue to lunge over the rocks on its way to the valleys below long after he had gone. The apricot trees would scrape out a spare existence and eventually die entirely apart from any consideration of his having passed that way. Only in that moment of the afternoon sun in Ladkh, as he abandoned thought of hurrying on to the monastery, did he receive back something he had unconsciously offered. Hence he declares, "The things that ignore us save us in the end. Their presence awakens silence in us; they refresh our courage with the purity of their detachment." Having become aware of a reality that exists entirely apart from the world of cares that keep him in turmoil, he was strangely set free. By its very act of ignoring him, the landscape invited him out of his frantic quest for self-fulfillment.[18]

Perhaps this is the great gift of mystery: It invites, but offers itself only to humility. We learn that there is nothing to attain: we take off our shoes and surrender.

---

16. Bruce Cockburn, "Mystery."
17. Webber, *Ancient-Future Faith*, 16.
18. Lane, *The Solace of Fierce Landscape*, 54.

Mystery

With its echoes found in the *apophatic* way, mystery reminds us that the spiritual life is founded in paradox. All is of grace; yet we must add our will and intention. God reveals himself to us: Yet the nearer we get to him to more we discover he is surrounded by cloud and thick darkness. In the face of mystery we have the opportunity not only to discover our smallness, but God's greatness. We discover that God does not ask to be analyzed, but loved. God is not a problem to be solved, but a person to be known. As Annie Dillard affirmed,

> Our life is a faint tracing on the surface of mystery. The surface of mystery is not smooth, any more than the planet is smooth, let alone a pine ... Forays into mystery cut bays and fine fjords, but the forested mainland itself is implacable both in its bulk and in its most filigreed fringe of detail. "Every religion that does not affirm that God is hidden," said Pascal flatly, "is not true."[19]

See also "God," "Epistemology," and "L'Avenir"

---

19. Dillard, *Pilgrim at Tinker Creek*, 147.

N

Narrative, Newbigin, New Monastic, Notae, and Nouwen

Narrative

> The Bible is fundamentally a story of a people's journey with God . . . In scripture we see that God is taking the disconnected elements of our lives and pulling them together into a coherent story that means something.[1]

> Neither revolution nor reformation can ultimately change a society, rather you must tell a new powerful tale, one so persuasive that it sweeps away the old myths and becomes the preferred story, one so inclusive that it gathers all the bits of our past and our present into a coherent whole, one that even shines some light into the future so that we can take the next step . . . If you want to change a society, then you have to tell an alternative story.[2]

If you want to change a society, tell an alternative story. The story of Jesus has transformed nations, and continues to transform them. Yet various attempts to disenchant the story have left it without the power it once had.

This loss isn't due to any lack in Jesus or any lack in the story itself. Rather the problem is ours; we reduced the scope of the story, depoliticized it, and made it and Jesus small enough for us to manage. The original story was about a stubborn people and an untamed God. We mythologized the story and removed its anchor in history, separating it from living memory. Then we shrank the story until it had no claim on our lives, but pointed

---

1. Hauerwas and Willimon, *Resident Aliens*, 53.
2. Quotiki, par. 1.

Narrative

only to a future kingdom divorced from the muck and mess of daily life. What power could that story possibly have? And what call to worship? Narrative does not exclude mystery, but actually invites it.

We neglected this narrative mode when our leaders became managers and technicians. Managers mostly rely on analysis, which is very useful for solving problems. The narrative mode is better suited for making sense. Analysis takes things apart; stories tell how things hang together. By staying with the narrative mode, people gather meaning instead of getting bogged down in details.

A narrative must be the possession of a living tradition, such that it invites us into a journey, and to participate with a people on a journey. Narrative that will move us connects to pilgrimage. "The Christian wayfarer, unlike the postmodern wanderer, is a disciple with a destination . . . a path."[3] Salvation is baptism into a new polis, a community that lives the story, forgetting its own worries in light of the destination, an adventure full of surprises and conflict, both comedy and tragedy, darkness and light. But whatever the daily character, the story is always visible in the lived community.

> It can only be that God begins in a small way, at one single place in the world. There must be a place . . . Visible, tangible . . . where the salvation of the world may begin: that is, where the world becomes what it is supposed to be according to God's plan. Beginning at that place, the new thing can spread abroad. All must have the chance to behold and test this new thing. Then, if they want to, they can allow themselves to be drawn into the story of salvation God is creating. Only in that way is freedom preserved.[4]

A place—where the world becomes what it is supposed to be. The kingdom is present, yet still to come. We live today in light of the future kingdom. A narrative that has meaning also has a *telos*, an end goal. The present is the end, and the future the means.

Newbigin talks about the grand story in one of his best known books.[5] He notes that reducing the story to propositions damages its integrity and limits its scope. Much of the challenge we face is abstraction, one of the legacies of modernity. We tried to distil the story to its essence,

---

3. Vanhoozer, "Pilgrim's Digress," 97.
4. Lohfink, *Does God Need the Church?*, 24.
5. Newbigin, *The Gospel in a Pluralist Society*, 12.

Narrative

reduce it to four simple points. That may have made it easier to grasp, but it also reduced its appeal to the intellect, without the heart. Clark Pinnock reminds us that theology has to orient itself to narrative, and not reduce story to a rulebook.[6]

M. Knight Shyamalan produces thrillers, but *Lady in the Water* has a different flavor.[7] The movie opens with line drawings that present some history. The world is split in two: One world is concerned with consumption and competition, the other with life, peace, and spirit. As the two paths diverge, there is loss of memory. Then the clincher: Man has forgotten how to listen.

Enter Mr. Heep, a doctor whose family was killed by a random act of violence, and who left his life and practice behind in an attempt to hide from the world and from his own grief. And then enter Story, a "Narf" from the Blue World, the forgotten world of water, where the other half of humankind still lives in peace. Story comes to meet a certain person who has a special destiny. When he meets her she prophesies his future and the meaning of his work. He remembers who he is and what he is called to do. He is empowered to meet the challenges of his vocation. Story reveals meaning, and also restores memory. She releases imagination, and thus enables a new future. But of course, none of this occurs without cost or without risk. And in the process an entire community discovers meaning and purpose. A group of individuals who had no apparent connection suddenly begin to act as a family.

What we can learn from these great stories is that life is risky, a grand adventure.[8] In a compelling story there is conflict and resistance. If there are no impediments along the way, then there is no chance of failure, and no character development. We identify with the great stories precisely because our heroes pay a cost, yet keep on moving. As Hauerwas and Willimon put it, "ethics is a function of the telos,"[9] a function of the larger story, the end to which the character is driven.

Near the end of the epic film *The Two Towers*, Sam and Frodo have a moment's peace after one of the nine riders has appeared to cast fear and doubt into the army of Gondor. Faramir has managed to repel the

---

6. Pinnock, *Tracking the Maze*, 182.
7. Shyamalan, *Lady in the Water*.
8. Urs von Balthasar gave us the concept of theodrama.
9. Hauerwas and Willimon, *Resident Aliens*, 61.

attack with an arrow to the neck of the huge bat-like animal that carries the Rider. As they stand in the ruins of the falling city, Sam talks to Frodo about the great stories, and how it often looks like the heroes won't make it, and when the path is so difficult we doubt that anyone could make the journey. Yet they keep on going, says Sam, because "There is some good in this world... and it's worth fighting for!"[10]

See also "Memory"

NEWBIGIN

> [The Gospel is] exclusive in the sense of affirming the unique truth in the revelation of Jesus Christ, but not in the sense of denying the possibility of salvation to those outside the Christian faith; inclusive in the sense of refusing to limit the saving grace of God to Christians, but not in the sense of viewing other religions as salvific; pluralist in the sense of acknowledging the gracious work of God in the lives of all human beings, but not in the sense of denying the unique and decisive nature of what God has done in Jesus Christ.[11]

In 1974, when Lesslie Newbigin returned home from missionary service in India, where he had been for nearly forty years, he "took up the challenge of trying to envision what a fresh encounter of the gospel with late-modern Western culture might look like."[12] Newbigin posed the question: "What would be involved in a missionary encounter between the gospel and this whole way of perceiving, thinking, and living that we call 'modern Western Culture'?"[13]

In 1983, Newbigin presented two major themes. First, that western culture is in crisis because it has too closely tied itself to an Enlightenment worldview. Secondly, the loss of influence the church has had within the culture. According to Newbigin, the church's voice has been marginalized in large part because it has surrendered its place in the public sphere and retreated into the private sector. Newbigin's concern was faithfulness, not

10. Jackson, *The Two Towers*.
11. Newbigin, *The Gospel in a Pluralist Society*, 182–83.
12. Van Gelder, *The Missional Church and Denominations*, 2.
13. Newbigin, *Foolishness to the Greeks*, 1.

a return to a position of worldly power. Newbigin clearly understood the limitations of the Christendom landscape.

Newbigin's missiology was formed both by practice, and by the mission theology that took shape within the International Missionary Council (IMC) conferences of the 1950s through the 1970s. One of the most significant of these was in Willingen, Germany in 1952. At Willingen it was recognized that the church could be neither the starting point nor the goal of mission. David Bosch notes, "God's salvific work precedes both the church and mission. We should not subordinate mission to the church nor the church to mission; both should, rather, be taken up into the *missio Dei*, which now became the overarching concept."[14] It was here that this idea (not the exact term) *missio Dei* first surfaced. Bosch further notes:

> Mission was understood as being derived from the very nature of God. It was thus put in the context of the doctrine on the *missio Dei* as God the Father sending the Son, and God the Father and the Son sending the Spirit was expanded to include yet another "movement": Father, Son, and Holy Spirit sending the church into the world. As far as missionary thinking was concerned, this linking with the doctrine of the Trinity constituted an important innovation. Willingen's image of mission was mission as participating in the sending of God.[15]

While the Trinitarian foundation for mission theology was later formulated by both Karl Hartenstein and Johannes Blauw, Newbigin articulated his own version. Central to Newbigin's understanding of mission is the work of the Triune God in calling and sending the church, empowered by the Spirit, into the world to participate fully in God's mission. It was Newbigin who made the now famous articulation of the church as a sign, foretaste, and an instrument of God's reign.

Newbigin's significance is found under three headings. First, his work served as the catalyst for bringing the issue of mission in western culture to the forefront of the agenda of mission studies. The appearance of his book *The Other Side of 1984* marks a major milestone for missiology.

Second, Newbigin played an active and central role in the International Missionary Council and the Commission of World Mission and Evangelism of the World Council of Churches. After serving as a mis-

---

14. Bosch, *Transforming Mission*, 370.
15. Ibid., 390.

sionary in India for twenty-three years, Newbigin took the post of general secretary of the IMC and then director of CWME of the WCC.

Finally, not only did he provide an impetus for renewed reflection on the issue of mission in western culture, he also worked on ecclesiological questions. The interface of those reflections, anchored in the real world of missionary praxis in the midst of a rapidly fading modernity, conditioned and nourished his rich theological work. His missionary ecclesiology has since been foundational for the ongoing engagement of the gospel with western culture.

See also "Bosch, David," "Missional," and "Post-Christendom"

NEW MONASTICISM

> The restoration of the church will surely come from a sort of new monasticism which has in common with the old only the uncompromising attitude of a life lived according to the sermon on the mount and the following of Christ. I believe it is now time to call people together to do this.[16]

The 24-7 Prayer International movement was birthed by Pete Greig, Andy Freeman, and friends around 2002 in Reading, England. At the time they were reading in the history of spirituality, with particular interest in the Celts, the desert fathers, and the monastic writers. Three years later they formally founded a missional order around their own rule of life: the Order of the Mustard Seed. Joining the Order requires a threefold vow of kindness, faithfulness to Christ, and missional living. The 24-7 prayer movement encourages involvement with marginalized people.

Jonathan Wilson is a part of the movement known as new monasticism. He closes his book *Living Faithfully* by describing four key characteristics:

1. A recovery of the gospel *telos* that sees the whole of life under the Lordship of Christ. This recovery will blur the distinction between the sacred and the secular.

---

16. Freeman and Greig, *Punk Monk*, 35.

2. It will be for the whole people of God. It will not divide the people of God into religious and secular vocations.

3. It will be disciplined [but] cannot simply be a recovery of the old monastic rules. The disciplines are always only a means to an end.

4. It will be undergirded by deep theological reflection and commitment. The purpose of the new monasticism is to provide the church with a means to recover its life and witness [mission] in the world... we must strive simultaneously for a recovery of right belief and right practice.[17]

Wilson underscores the counter cultural nature of the people of God in this world. He affirms that "we are constantly tempted to form a church that will simply undergird the civil order. A new monasticism refuses that temptation... The new monasticism envisioned here is the form by which the church will recover its *telos*, the living tradition of the gospel, the practices and virtues that sustain that faithfulness, and the community marked by faithful living in a fragmented world."[18]

Notae

> The creedal "marks" of the church are [not] wrong, but... not exhaustive. When interpreted in absolute and exclusive terms, noting the unity, holiness, catholicity and apostolicity of the church may in fact be misleading; these may actually mark forms of religious community that have little to do with Jesus' way of knowing, acting and being in the world.[19]

In LeRon's words I hear echoes (probably not intentional) of Howard Snyder's work where he recalls the Council of Nicaea.[20] At that time the council (however Constantinian, it was a genuine theological conversation) declared that the church is *one, holy, catholic, apostolic*... but these

---

17. Ibid., 72–76.
18. Ibid., 78.
19. Shults, "Reforming Ecclesiology in Emerging Churches," 16.
20. Snyder, *Decoding the Church*, 22.

terms themselves remain ambiguous. Using the analogy of DNA (always paired strings) Snyder argues that the New Testament reveals the missing pairs. He spends a good portion of space working out these details. For Snyder the church is:

1. Diverse as well as one
2. Charismatic as well as holy
3. Local as well as catholic or universal
4. Prophetic as well as apostolic[21]

In the modern world, the western church sacrificed its diversity, was often legalistic rather than grace centered, often neglected the living presence of the Spirit in empowered ministry, and gave up its prophetic role. Furthermore, it was often hierarchical, (from Latin *hieros* for priest) placing men in positions of power rather than mutually submitting to the active presence of a living head. It is possible to have all the classical marks of the church yet be essentially apostate, Pelagian, Gnostic or Deistic. A lack of diversity is a good indicator that we have stopped responding to the Spirit, who is continually creative and who loves diversity: just look at snowflakes, flowers, a sunset or the world of mammals, much less the microscopic world.

Late in 2008, Andy Rowell posted some reflections on notae or "marks of the church," guessing at where a selection of sixty theologians would fall in terms of high to low ecclesiologies.[22] Andy included Rowan Williams, the Anglican Archbishop, and even John Howard Yoder. Williams denoted the essential characteristics as:

1. Moral discernment oriented by martyrdom
2. Participation in the sacraments
3. Standing under the authority of Scripture
4. Communicating the Good News drawn from a letter[23]

---

21. Ibid.
22. Rowell, "60 Theologians."
23. Ibid.

Yoder, on the other hand, was less interested in the essentials than in characteristics of a thriving community, echoing the ethos of the later church health movement.

Other popular writers on the gospel and culture have been more concerned to map the essential qualities of God's people around their nature as a sent people. This would have met the approval of Karl Barth, no less Lesslie Newbigin or David Bosch. Barth notes, "As an apostolic Church the Church can never in any respect be an end in itself, but, following the existence of the apostles, it exists only as it exercises the ministry of a herald."[24]

Alan Hirsch echoed this sentiment by arguing that the DNA of the church is always missional: thus, mDNA.[25] For Hirsch, mDNA represents the "apostolic genius" of the church. He outlines six elements:

1. Jesus is Lord
2. Disciple Making
3. Missional—Incarnational Impulse
4. Apostolic Environment
5. Organic Systems
6. *Communitas* instead of community

This is a unique list because it recognizes and pulls context into the conversation. It is less a "marks of the church" question than a "marks of the postmodern church on mission" kind of list, with a very strong anchor in systems and complexity frameworks.

Jesus is Lord is a confessional stance, but begs the Trinitarian question. Hirsch was making the political point in the context of the first century church. To confess Jesus is Lord was to claim an alternative allegiance. In the Addendum of the book an appeal is made for the passion and fire of Pentecostalism: the Holy Spirit appears in a discussion of chaos and adaptive and self-organizing structures.

In his appeal to *communitas* instead of community, Hirsch was making the point that the church is a special kind of community, formed around shared purpose and living in the tension of an alternative kingdom.

---

24. Barth, *Church Dogmatics*, 724.
25. Hirsch, *The Forgotten Ways*, 271.

See also "Communitas," "God," and "Missional"

Nouwen, Henri

Born in Nijkerk, Holland, on January 24, 1932, Henri Nouwen felt called to the priesthood at a very young age. He was ordained in 1957 as a diocesan priest and studied psychology at the Catholic University of Nijmegen. In 1964 he moved to the United States to study at the Menninger Clinic. He went on to teach at the University of Notre Dame, and the Divinity Schools of Yale and Harvard. For several months during the 70s, Nouwen lived and worked with the Trappist monks in the Abbey of the Genesee,[26] and in the early eighties he lived with the poor in Peru. This is also when he met Jean Vanier. At the time Henri was struggling with the pace of his life, often feeling empty and alone. His popularity was growing and he was increasingly in demand as a public speaker and teacher, but he found this role and its demands unfulfilling. He began to suspect that he was neglecting an inner call, and when he met Vanier he realized that in the simplicity and obscurity of working with the mentally handicapped he might meet Christ in a new way.[27]

> I believe you can look at solitude, community, and ministry as three disciplines by which we create space for God. If we create space in which God can act and speak, something surprising will happen. You and I are called to these disciplines if we want to be disciples.[28]

In 1985 he was called to join L'Arche in Trosly, France, the first of over a hundred communities founded by Jean Vanier where people with developmental disabilities live with assistants. A year later Nouwen came to make his home at L'Arche Daybreak near Toronto, Canada. He died suddenly on September 21st, 1996, in Holland and is buried in King City, Ontario.

Nouwen wrote more than forty books on the spiritual life. He corresponded regularly in English, Dutch, German, French, and Spanish with hundreds of friends and reached out to thousands through his Eucharistic

---

26. He relates this story in *The Genesee Diary*.
27. He tells his story in detail in, *In the Name of Jesus*.
28. Nouwen, "From Solitude to Community to Ministry," 1.

celebrations, lectures, and retreats. Nouwen believed that what is most personal is most universal; he wrote, "By giving words to these intimate experiences I can make my life available to others."

Nouwen's warm and vulnerable pastoral theology has provided an anchor for many who suspected that modernity and its effects were numbing the spirit, and destroying some of the most beautiful gifts of Christian faith. His insight, especially when applied to leadership, was often intensely challenging to the status quo. Of success he writes:

> There is a great difference between successful and fruitfulness. Success comes from strength, control, and respectability. A successful person has the energy to create something, to keep control over its development, and to make it available in large quantities. Success brings many rewards and often fame. Fruits, however, come from weakness and vulnerability. And fruits are unique. A child is the fruit conceived in vulnerability, community is the fruit born through shared brokenness, and intimacy is the fruit that grows through touching one another's wounds. Let's remind one another that what brings us true joy is not successfulness but fruitfulness.[29]

And of power he writes,

> One thing is clear to me:
> The temptation of power is greatest when intimacy is a threat.
> Much Christian leadership is exercised by people
> who do not know how to develop healthy, intimate relationships
> and have opted for power and control instead.
> Many Christian empire-builders
> have been people unable to give and receive love.[30]

See also "Formation, Spiritual," "Hospitality," and "Leadership"

---

29. Nouwen, *Lifesigns*, 41.
30. Nouwen, *In the Name of Jesus*, 77.

Obedience, Office (The), and Orthodoxy

OBEDIENCE

Following Jesus is an experiential thing because we have a living teacher who speaks. "My sheep hear my voice."[1] So the will of God is not something we figure out in a strategic sense but requires personal intimacy and corporate discipline—a daily lived obedience. It is no accident that renewal movements often include charismatic elements and stories of divine guidance. Perhaps *charism* and *covenant* are a double helix: the best interweave of word and Spirit.

At the heart of a covenant community is an intentional agreement between its members to live in a certain way. Sometimes this way is described by an order or rule of life (the word derives from the Latin *regula* which means rhythm, regularity of pattern). Rule in our place in history tends to sound oppressive and limiting, but a rule is not an end, but a means to an end.[2] Henri Nouwen writes that, "A Rule offers 'creative boundaries within which God's loving presence can be recognized and celebrated.' It does not prescribe but invite, it does not force but guide, it does not threaten but warn, it does not instill fear but points to love. In this it is a call to freedom, freedom to love."[3] In Paul Hiebert's terms

---

1. John 10.

2. Somewhere Saint Gregory writes that we always live with the danger of transforming supplies for the journey into hindrances to our arrival. A rule is a good thing if it deepens our walk and lightens our path.

3. Found at the Northumbria community website. Similarly, Newbigin writes, "true freedom is found not by seeking to develop the powers of the self...but [in] true relatedness in love and obedience." *Foolishness to the Greeks*, 119.

covenant communities share the characteristics of both *centered sets and bounded sets*.[4]

It's at this point that questions of governance arise. Many communities in our day are actually built around charismatic leaders more than shared purpose. But this makes the community very fragile. It seems we have a choice to build leadership cults, or a leadership *culture*.[5]

Historically communities oriented around a common rule have identified people in their midst who are unusual for their wisdom. According to Lawrence M. Miller[6] the key to holding together diverse communities of leadership types is the synergist. Miller describes a synergist as "a leader who has escaped his or her own conditioned tendencies toward one style and incorporated, appreciated and unified each of the styles of leadership on the life-cycle curve."[7] The synergist guards the ethos and her role is to foster and maintain a creative and open space within the team so that no one role dominates.[8] She helps maintain clarity of vision and her investment is in internal capital. Older traditions call this person an abbot or abbess.

The believer's church has a special legacy with regard to leadership and community, understanding leadership as primarily a spiritual vocation. In the last generation, under the hegemony of modernity, we nearly lost this, and we have work to do to unlearn a professional model of ministry and relearn a vocational model. Sandra Cronk talks about this same struggle within the *Society of Friends*:

> The professional model assumes that ministry is primarily a skill or body of knowledge that is offered to recipients. These skills are part of a job. But in earlier years Friends saw ministry much more as a way of being and relating. Ministers were recognized for their skills, to be sure, but they were leaders more because their whole way of being pointed toward God or conveyed God's love and caring. Their words, actions and relationships were their ministry. In

---

4. These concepts come from the work of Paul Hiebert and appear in various sources, such as Guder et al, *Missional Church*.

5. Deering et al., "Leadership Cults and Culture."

6. Miller, *Barbarians to Bureaucrats*.

7. "Organizational Life-Cycles and Management Styles."

8. The domination of certain leadership types has been ironically designated the *sola pastora* model, but the loss of diversity is no laughing matter. Biologists know that genetic diversity is what allows organisms to survive under rapidly changing conditions.

Obedience

this old Quaker conception, *ministry is not just a matter of doing but of being.*

There are problems with the kind of structure which compartmentalizes life into private and professional spheres. This kind of division tends to make ministry a task. It prevents a full relationship with another human being in which redemption can happen.[9]

It won't be an easy task to recover this older model, because we have seen so many abuses of spiritual authority. Given our negative experience with authority and the fear generated from these, we have work to do to rebuild trust.[10]

A covenant structure embeds authority, and the first expression of authority is mutuality. Triads are the space where we hold one another accountable for the commitments we have made, and learn the discipline of confession and forgiveness. Face to face is where the kind of space can grow that allows us to genuinely unburden ourselves, relearn trust, confess to one another, and heal. Bonhoeffer writes, "The desire we so often hear today for 'episcopal figures' . . . springs from a spiritually sick need for the admiration of men . . . because the genuine authority of service appears so unimpressive."[11] Later he writes, "The question of trust . . . is determined by faithfulness to the service of Jesus Christ . . . never by the extraordinary talents [one] possesses. Pastoral authority is attained only . . . by the brother among brothers."[12]

Abbots and spiritual directors are nothing new, just something old that we misplaced. In the early days of the church elders were given honour and authority through their sacrifice and their care for the flock. During the industrial age this role was increasingly awarded to competent managers as churches were increasingly imagined and run as corporations.[13] More recently the role has been professionalized.

---

9. Cronk, "Discovering and Nurturing Ministers," 8.

10. See Sargent's summary of the five core needs for transformation. In Koch, *Finding Authentic Hope and Wholeness*. The core needs are: *security* (who can I trust?), which involves freedom from fear, anxiety, danger, doubt, *identity* (who am I?); the characteristics and qualities of a person, *belonging* (who wants me?).

11. Bonhoeffer, *Life Together*, 109.

12. Ibid.

13. See in particular the discussion on the evolution of the clergy, Darell, *Missional Church*, 190–99.

As a result, those whose gift is to guide, shepherd, and care for people find themselves marginalized, and the communities in which they live are a kind of soil that does not produce mature and healthy spiritual leaders. Consequently, leaders who attempt to function as spiritual guides often lack either the freedom or the necessary experience and maturity. We continue to have spiritual elders among us, but they are too few and often unrecognized, and rarely occupy official positions. Even when office and person are congruent, systemic issues limit healthy functioning. The body has suffered as a result.

In a book penned in the 60s, Gordon Cosby detailed the three types of relationships we need in order to keep growing. We need those who are further along the way; we need peers and fellow pilgrims; and we need those who are not as advanced as we are—a little flock to tend and nourish.

> Gordon asked, "What feelings get evoked in you when the call to be a spiritual director is extended?" What did Christ mean when he said, "Feed my sheep." Who did he mean to do it? and when?
>
> Most of the class responded, "I can't be a spiritual director. I need one." Gordon emphasized the vital need for assuming this responsibility for another if we were to know any vivid sense of Christ's presence. "It is so basic," he said, "that unless we deal with this call in our lives, we will reach a point beyond which we cannot go. Feeding and tending others is basic to our lives as Christians."[14]

See also "Benedict, Saint" and "Rule"

Office, The

When we live from a still center we tend to see life differently. This is because life lived from the center engages our whole being and the lenses through which we see are not as blurred by our own anxieties. But living from the center in a hurried and harried world is not an easy task; and in our market culture sometimes it seems nearly impossible. Simon Carey Holt writes:

14. O'Connor, *Journey Inward, Journey Outward*, 112.

Office, The

> Skimming the surface is the best I can do sometimes. Though I crave depth—the leisure of lingering in one place, one conversation, one task, one thought—the pace of the day doesn't always allow it. Such is life . . . I know that. But I know myself too; I can only skim the surface for so long. My spirit begins to crumble at the edges.[15]

Simon holds hope that our homes can become places of healing and retreat, yet so often they seem to be the opposite: places of more busyness and activity.

Around 2005, I discovered the daily Office. As I began to enter its rhythms I began learning some things:

1. I noticed a growing interest in patterns of prayer among some of my friends.
2. I realized that my spontaneous prayer life lacks discipline.
3. I was looking for a connection with a larger story and tradition—I didn't want to reinvent the wheel.
4. I realized a pattern / tradition of prayer might be helpful, especially one that was tested through time.
5. I began to love the rhythm and language of the prayers.

The Office, or canonical hours, has been around since the fourth century and is practiced by monastic groups, and within the Catholic, Orthodox, and Anglican communities. This means that well over a hundred million people follow this rhythm. The practice of daily prayers grew from the Jewish practice of reciting prayers at set times of the day and was adopted by the early church.

In the Book of Acts, Peter and John visit the Temple for the afternoon prayers (Acts 3:1). Psalm 119:164 states: "Seven times a day I praise you for your righteous laws." Canonical hours are ancient divisions of time, developed by the Christian church, serving as increments between the prescribed prayers of the daily round. A Book of Hours contains such a set of prayers.

Choosing a particular discipline and then working it with others is one response to fragmentation and analysis paralysis. There are so many options out there, and so many distractions. Unless we choose a practice

---

15. Holt, *"Time Away."*

together we do not grow in it or we simply give up. But the practice is only a means to an end. "[A discipline is] any activity within our power that we engage in to enable us to do what we cannot do by direct effort."[16]

See also "Rhythm" and "Rule"

ORTHODOXY

> Orthodoxy in the older and original Christian sense meant "correct praise" or "right worship." The early church's stress was on faith, not so much as an intellectual assent to doctrinal propositions, but as a way of living in the graced community of an actual assembly at worship before the living God.[17]

Orthodoxy hasn't been a prominent theme in conversations among missional and emergent leaders so much as *orthopraxy*. But at least one prominent leader recently used the word 'orthodoxy' in a book title: Brian McLaren. McLaren chooses an unusual subtitle: *Why I am a missional, evangelical, post/protestant, liberal/conservative, mystical/poetic, . . . unfinished Christian*. In the chapter "Why I Am Incarnational," McLaren writes,

> I originally entitled this chapter, "Why I Am Buddhist/Muslim/Hindu/Jewish." The original title proved excessively provocative, if not downright misleading. So the current title emerged, affirming that a generous orthodoxy takes the incarnation very seriously, affirming that God's movement "us-ward" in Jesus sends us on a similar trajectory "them-ward."
>
> Because I follow Jesus, then, I am bound to Jews, Muslims, Buddhists, Hindus, agnostics, atheists, NewAgers, everyone (religious broadcasters, I was just reminded by a still, small voice) not only am I bound to them in love, but I am also actually called to . . . in some real sense (please don't minimize this before you qualify it) become one of them, to enter their world and be with them in it.[18]

---

16. Willard, "Live Life to the Full," 1.
17. Clapp, *A Peculiar People*, 120.
18. McLaren, *A Generous Orthodoxy*, 250.

Orthodoxy

So this movement becomes one more attempt at genuinely embracing "the other." That's helpful, because too often orthodoxy has been about guarding borders, testing who is in and who is out. At its worst it became an inhuman and religious exercise.

Perhaps orthodoxy is an *event*, in the Derridean sense. That is, *orthodoxy happens* when human beings get together and practice it (talk about God, worship God, pray to God, write books about God). There's no orthodoxy somewhere out there that one can point to and say: See that? That's orthodoxy. That's what we're trying to get to.

David Fitch writes on the authority of Scripture.

> [Inerrancy] is the question for we who seek to remain evangelical in these times, or for we who maybe don't care about being evangelical but wish to maintain a high view of Scripture . . . Stanley Hauerwas, when asked in an interview, "what do you mean when you say the Bible is true?" Stanley replied, "I mean *I would die for it.*" He then reminded us that the word "witness" to the truth comes from the Greek root, *martyrion*, or martyr. Perhaps this is the next fruitful direction towards a strategy for defining the authority of Scripture in the world. When we say the Bible is true, we believe it sufficiently, live it so absolutely, that we'd be willing to die for it.
>
> This of course implies that the Scriptures be embodied in a community, where its ways of life and language can only be understood together . . . There are those who say, "I don't want the truth of Scripture depending on people actually living it." That in itself is telling. But I believe this way promises to provide the means to describe both a way to talk about truthfulness as well as a way to define Scripture as apostolic, given by God through the prophets and Jesus Christ and His apostles, to be carried in a people, protected and enlivened by the Holy Spirit until Christ returns. This way is unassailable in these postmodern times and becomes the means for God through his people to call the world to Christ, the way, the truth and the life.[19]

---

19. Fitch, "I'm Willing to Die for it."

P

Paradox and Post-Christendom

Paradox

> At the still point of the turning world. Neither flesh nor fleshless;
> Neither from nor towards; at the still point, there the dance is,
> But neither arrest nor movement.[1]

Paradox has become a common word in the missional conversation. In part this is because the death of modernity has meant a recovery of mystery. But in part it is a recognition of complexity, and that change and growth in this suddenly mysterious world involves paradox.

In the west our churches have sought control, boxing God and setting him at our service, or marketing him as a product for consumption. Pete Rollins responds to this modern idolatry. He proclaims doubt as a virtue, and notes that what we often consider definitions are actually non-definitions. Rollins quotes Anselm: "Therefore, Lord, you are not merely that than which a greater cannot be though, you are something greater than can be thought," and Saint Leo: "Even if one has progressed far in divine things, one is never nearer the truth than when one understands that those things still remain to be discovered."[2] Mystical theology is paradoxical.

Paradox is a function of the limits of language and human knowledge. "The desire to get beyond language forces us to stretch language

---

1. T. S. Eliot, "Burnt Norton II."
2. Rollins, *How (Not) to Speak of God*, 27.

Paradox

to its very limits ... in order to tear through them and glimpse what lies beneath."[3] The desire to say nothing opens up creative space.

But more: Paradox is a requirement for change. Bill Buker quotes Keeney that, "The deepest order of change is epistemological change."[4] He talks about first order change, which is common sense change. This is the kind of change that happens when your spouse has to cut back at work. It will mean an adjustment in your family. Either you spend less, or someone else works more.

This works fine when there aren't powerful personal and psychological dynamics involved. However, when someone has become dependent on something and it shapes their very identity, this first order strategy will not succeed.

The second order of change involves becoming open to reevaluating the presuppositions that govern first order strategies. This is usually experienced as a crisis and one's world-view may be in shambles. Then comes the clincher:

> In comparison with the rules and premises that previously governed their system, these new ones often seem paradoxical in nature. Instead of the commonsense idea that out of control drinking should be addressed by choosing in-control behavior, second-order change says that the complementary position of honesty is better. Instead of continuing to engage in the first-order strategy of exerting more willpower in a determined effort to prove their control over alcohol, it becomes important for alcoholics to recognize and admit that they are [powerless.] To genuinely make this admission, a shift in self-perception is required. Rather than exulting in pride, bowing in humility becomes appropriate. Such a change is generally made possible through the gift of hitting bottom.[5]

This is highly relevant stuff, because we are faced in our time with a world that is complex beyond our imaginations. Living in this world requires an ability to embrace ambiguity.

Because we are finite beings, even God's self-revelation is mysterious. One of the oldest frameworks for thinking about spirituality was first articulated by Gregory of Nyssa. Gregory characterized growth in faith as entry into a moonlit desert night, then movement to a fog covered moun-

---

3. Ibid., 42.
4. Buker, "Spiritual Development and the Epistemology of Systems Theory," 144.
5. Ibid.

tain, and finally into the impenetrable darkness of a thick cloud (Moses on the mountain). The more darkness faith could embrace, he thought, the greater the light it gave. This is classic apophatic expression, the *via negativa* as compared to *via positiva*. We need both perspectives if we are to honour the weakness and foolishness of the Cross.

> See also "Apophatic," "Mystery," "Epistemology," "Saint Gregory," and "Theopoetics"

Post-Christendom (Post-Colonial, Post-Evangelical, Postmodern, Post-Secular)

As the list of "posts" continues to grow, it's reasonable to ask if all these post-words are necessary. But there are a few posts other than postmodern that deserve attention.

Since Foucault, we are forced to examine the way we use power. It's true that this should have been obvious to us from the incarnation itself: Paul makes it clear in his hymn in Philippians 2 that the self-emptying of God is completely subversive. In the gospel, power structures are turned topsy-turvy. The wisdom of the wise becomes foolishness. That the Creator Himself should take up a tower and wash our feet—to quote Teviah, it's "unthinkable, impossible, absurd!"

Post-Christendom, we are forced to think about the advantages and disadvantages of power. When Constantine declared a national religion, merging (in theory) two distinct kingdoms, the gospel itself was distorted. The voluntary component, and the necessity of a journey with all its attendant risks, ceased to exist. Suddenly all cats were grey. And from that place of enforced clarity, the story itself became a totalizing narrative, though maybe this wasn't so obvious before the crusades or the inquisition. No, that wasn't the world God intended. The gospel Jesus preached offered the possibility that we could reject Him.

Stuart Murray helps with a definition: "Post-Christendom is the culture that emerges as the Christian faith loses coherence within a society that has been definitively shaped by the Christian story and as the

Post-Christendom

institutions that have been developed to express Christian convictions decline in influence."[6] He continues.

> Post-Christendom can easily be perceived as a threat and associated with failure and decline. Our response to the challenges it presents may be to burrow ostrich-like into the remaining sand of familiar church culture, scan the horizon for growing churches that claim we can continue doing what we have always done, or clutch desperately at promises of revival or programs that promise to restore our fortunes. Indeed, the more we understand post-Christendom, the greater may be the temptation to respond in such ways: post-Christendom is not an easy environment for discipleship, mission or church.[7]

It all looks very different from the margins. We can grieve the loss of our privileged position, or remember that foolishness always defined the way of the cross. Moreover, when we forsake our allegiance with the mighty in this world, we rediscover a place of dependence on God. Robert Capon writes, "Marginality, in short, leaves the church free, if it is faithful, to cherish its absurdity; establishment just makes it fall in love all over again with the irrelevant respectability of the world's wisdom and power."[8]

Obviating the things we lost in our eagerness to be respectable, we discover a new humility. This might translate into a renewed listening posture. Too often we have acted as if the truth . . . even God . . . is in our pockets. (Like some twisted Gollum: What does it have in its pocketses?) Adopting a posture of humility makes us more human, more approachable, more willing to listen and learn and to meet others as equals. Samir Selmanovic writes,

> If we believe that the ultimate method of spreading the Good News is through loving people, why do non-Christians so rarely feel loved by Christians? My thesis is that love accepts what others have to offer and we think non-Christians don't have much of anything to add to what is really valuable to us, namely the gospel. Although we accept their virtues with admiration and their brokenness with compassion, we do not seriously expect them to add to what matters most to us—our knowledge of and our relation-

---

6. Ibid., 10.
7. Ibid., 11.
8. Capon, *The Astonished Heart*, 64.

ship with God. We withhold from them the possibility of being our teachers. Without an attitude of learning, we have not entered a sacred "I/Thou" relationship. And that's why they hold back. The world is withholding from us what we are withholding from the world.[9]

So much more could be said, but we have other "posts" to roast. Dave Tomlinson writes, "a young woman told me, 'Evangelicalism helped me to begin with, but now I feel I've outgrown it.' Arrogant? Possibly, yet she was voicing something which cropped up continually in my conversations with people: the feeling that evangelicalism is extremely good at introducing people to faith in Christ, but distinctly unhelpful when it comes to ... progressing."[10]

Not surprising, since conversion in evangelicalism has too often been reduced to confessing belief and praying a prayer. Where to go after that? "Heaven is my home; I'm just passing through." Not much incentive for discipleship or to change the world if this is all just a short blip on God's radar.

To be post-evangelical is to present a critique of evangelicalism.[11] That critique includes a critique of individualism and anti-intellectualism, and also a critique of materialism and the attendant consumerism. For many, to be post-evangelical is to embrace a nuanced approach to politics, with an inclination to be neither red nor blue but somewhere in between. Finally, while many post-evangelicals embrace the authority of Scripture, most refute a particular philosophical articulation of inerrancy.[12]

Stan Grenz suggests that postmodernity may have been born in Canada in 1979 when the Conseil des Universites of the government of Quebec requested a report on "knowledge in the most highly developed societies."[13] They turned to Jean-Francios Lyotard, a French philosopher from the Institute Polytechnique de Philosophie of the University of Paris. Lyotard responded with a short piece titled *The Postmodern Condition: A Report on Knowledge*. Lyotard's work did not initiate the discussion so much as making it accessible.

---

9. Selmanovic, "The Sweet Problem of Inclusiveness," 189–99.
10. Tomlinson, *The Post-Evangelical*, 10.
11. Perriman, "What is post-evangelicalism?"
12. McKnight, "The Ironic Faith of Emergents."
13. Grenz, *A Primer on Postmodernism*, 29.

Post-Christendom

So what is the postmodern condition? John Franke writes,

> Broadly speaking the term postmodern implies the rejection of certain central features of the modern project, such as its quest for certain, objective and universal knowledge, along with its dualism and its assumption of the inherent goodness of knowledge. It is this critical agenda, rather than any proposed constructive paradigm to replace the modern vision, that unites postmodern thinkers.[14]

More specifically, the postmodern view abandons the notion of an objective world, rejecting a "realist" understanding of knowledge and truth in favor of a non-realist understanding. Grenz writes, "we have moved from an objectivist to a constructivist outlook."[15] Postmodern thinkers argue that we do not simply encounter a world that is "out there," but rather that we construct the world with language. "There is no fixed vantage point beyond our own structuring of the world from which to gain a purely objective view of reality."[16]

Similarly, Kevin Vanhoozer reviews the postmodern condition with reference to Lyotard as incredulity towards metanarratives. He writes,

> We cannot believe in the "one true story" that explains every other story. We are too aware that other groups have their own stories that claim to be equally comprehensive. Metanarratives thus dwindle into mere narratives; "reason" is situated, deuniversalized.[17]

Post-secular is a term that is gaining currency. It seems particularly prominent within the conversation known as radical orthodoxy. Amos Yong comments on James Smith's representation of the theological conversation labelled radical orthodoxy (RO). Yong writes,

> RO mounts a five-pronged offensive meant in part to usher in a post-secular space. First, RO criticizes modernity's individualism, liberalism, and dualism . . . Second . . . if there is no autonomous reason, then there is no purely secular space within which such reason operates. The result is a reconciliation of faith and reason which modernity had segregated. Third . . . if there is no purely

---

14. Franke, "*Reforming Theology,*" 9.
15. Grenz, *A Primer,* 40.
16. Ibid., 41.
17. Op Cit., 87.

secular space, then the boundaries between the secular and the sacred are also removed.[18]

James K. A. Smith identifies Saint Augustine as a crucial resource for a post-secular theology. He comments:

> There is a sense in which Augustine's cultural situation mirrors our own postmodern predicament. As Ward observes, "It seems to me we stand, culturally, in a certain relation to Augustine's thinking . . . Poised as he was on the threshold between radical pluralism (which he called paganism) and the rise of Christendom, we stand on the other side of that history: at the end of Christendom and the reemergence of radical (as distinct from liberal) pluralism." Like Augustine, we are constructing theology and engaging in Christian witness in the shadow of both a dominant empire and a religious pluralism.
>
> Third, the substance of Augustine's thought—in particular his epistemology, his cultural analysis, and his theological vision—resonates with the postfoundationalist project that rejects the autonomy of reason and hence also the autonomy of the sociopolitical sphere. In short, for Augustine there is no secular, non-religious sphere as construed by modernity; there is only paganism or true worship.[19]

See also "Epistemology" and "Hermeneutics"

PRACTICES (*See "New Monasticism" and "Rhythm"*)

---

18. Yong, "Radically Orthodox," 233–50.
19. Smith, *Introducing Radical Orthodoxy*, 46–47.

Rhythm and Rule

Rhythm

Christine Sine made the point that natural rhythms are all around us. Sunrise, sunset; fall, winter, spring; day, and night; the tides wax and wane; our hearts beat with regularity; even at the molecular level there is rhythm.[1]

It's no different in the Scripture. Eugene Peterson demonstrates the rhythms expressed by the writer of Genesis (67). There is a rhythm to creation and Sabbath, and at the textual level the author has developed a careful structure, represented in the numbering of the days. Initially the rhythm is 123456777, but in the second account becomes 1,2,3/3,4,5,6/6, 7/7/7. Even the structure of the writing carries a message. The clues are in the cadence, and when the writing was read aloud (as intended) Peterson pictures the listeners tapping their feet. The threesome of sevens is like the tag line we repeat at the end of a song.[2]

What happens when we remove rhythm from our daily lives? What happens when we become a-rhythmic in our shared lives? Many of our faith communities have become attractional—centred on a gathering and even abstracted from the soil they grow in. They neglected the fundamental rhythm of gathering and dispersion, worship and witness and something went wrong.

Rhythms are so close to us that they are transparent: the rhythm of the flow of blood within our bodies. The life is in the blood. Blood is the means of transportation for food and oxygen and bodily defences.

---

1. Sine, "We've Got Rhythm."
2. Peterson, *Christ Plays in Ten Thousand Places*, 67.

The blood receives oxygen and food and is pumped outward by the heart muscle. When it has done its work, it moves inward for cleansing and nourishment then it is pumped outward again. This inward and outward rhythm is not optional. When the rhythm ends, so does life!

French psychiatrist David Servan-Schreiber has recently introduced new treatments that are making Freud and Prozac obsolete. The treatments seem most powerful against two of the most common maladies of our time: anxiety disorders and depression. How fascinating that the treatments are related to natural rhythms. His discovery? There is a powerful connection between the heart and the brain. A coherent heart rhythm is able to bring the emotional brain to rest. When your heart is beating in a healthy way, you can heal stress, depression, and other mental afflictions.[3]

Similarly, we need encouragement, prayer, information, and sometimes correction. We need to love and be loved. And then we need to take that love out into the world, partnering with God in the redemption of His good creation.

Some argue that ecclesial rhythms could be spontaneous, similar in kind to the distributed faith models Barna describes in *Revolution*.[4] But those models are difficult to maintain in the fragmented world most of us experience, where there are so many demands on our time and we participate in multiple communities. Distributed faith affirms choice, but it also reinforces a secular understanding of freedom where the self is the centre. It places us back into the conundrum of analysis paralysis: What do I choose and why? And it tends to neglect hospitality, genuinely welcoming the other, in favour of hanging with safe and clean people.

The answer of the Celtic monasteries to the need of their day was *roots, rhythms, and relationship*. Could a new call to simplicity, friendship, stability, mission and attention to God . . . *lectio and opus Dei* . . . a new monastic movement, built around covenanted rhythms help us to rediscover the meaning of the Body? Could it assist us in forming faithful communities of Jesus apprentices, a community of friends on a missional journey together?

There is much to be said for spontaneity, but faith communities need to establish rhythm in their practices, or they will have difficulty

---

3. Touber, "Our Natural Instinct to Heal," 36–40.
4. Barna, *Revolution*.

maintaining coherence. Fragmentation will continue to plague them, and non-covenantal reality will result in distractions and negotiations that contribute to stress and *arhythmia*. Escaping the vestiges of the duality of sacred and secular life, the duality of theory and practice, will require us to rediscover essential rhythms.

See also "Benedict, Saint" and "New Monasticism"

Romantic Theology (*see "Theopoetics"*)

Rule

Faith communities built around shared rhythms structure their lives with a *rule*. A rule is a spiritual rather than a legislative document. It is 'simply a handbook to make the radical demands of the gospel a practical reality in daily life.

> A Rule offers "creative boundaries within which God's loving presence can be recognized and celebrated." It does not prescribe but invite, it does not force but guide, it does not threaten but warn, it does not instil fear but points to love. In this it is a call to freedom, freedom to love.[5]

The website of the Northumbria community reads:

> The word "rule" has bad connotations for many, implying restrictions, limitations and legalistic attitudes. But a Rule is essentially about *freedom*. It helps us to stay centered, bringing perspective and clarity to the way of life to which God has called us. The word derives from the Latin "regula" which means "rhythm, regularity of pattern, a recognizable standard" for the conduct of life. "Regula" is a feminine noun which carried gentle connotations rather than the harsh negatives that we often associate with the phrase "rules and regulations" today. We do not want to be legalistic. A Rule is an orderly way of existence but we embrace it as a way of life not as keeping a list of rules. It is a means to an end—and the end is that we might seek God with authenticity and live more effectively for Him.[6]

See also "Benedict, Saint," "Formation, Spiritual," and "New-Monasticism"

---

5. Nouwen, "The Rule—Briefly."
6. Raine, "The Rule—Deeper."

S

Sacramental, and Social Imaginary

SACRED/SECULAR (*see "Post-Secular"*)

SACRAMENTAL

In *Holy the Firm* Annie Dillard writes,

> I'm out on the road again walking, and toting a backload of God.
> Here is a bottle of wine with a label, Christ with a cork. I bear holiness splintered into a vessel, very God of very God, the sempiternal silence personal and brooding, bright on the back of my ribs. I start up the hill.
> The world is changing. The landscape begins to respond as a current upwells. It is starting to clack with itself, though nothing moves in space and there's no wind. It is starting to utter its infinite particulars, each overlapping and lone, like a hundred hills of hounds all giving tongue. The hedgerows are blackberry brambles, white snowberries, red rose hips, gaunt and clattering broom. Their leafless stems are starting to live visibly deep in their centers, as hidden as banked fires live, and as clearly as recognition, mute, shines forth from eyes. Above me the mountains are raw nerves, sensible and exultant; the trees, the grass, and the asphalt below me are living petals of mind, each sharp and invisible, held in a greeting or glance full perfectly formed. There is something stretched or jostling about the sky which, when I study it, vanishes. Why are there all these apples in the world, and why so wet and transparent? Through all my clothing, through

the pack on my back and through the bottle's glass I feel the wine. Walking faster and faster, weightless, I feel the wine. It sheds light in slats through my rib cage, and fills the buttressed vaults of my ribs with light pooled and buoyant. I am moth; I am light. I am prayer and I can hardly see.[1]

A sacrament is an outward and physical sign of an inward and spiritual grace. The Catholic Encyclopedia describes it like this: "We can say that the whole world is a vast sacramental system, in that material things are unto men the signs of things spiritual and sacred, even of the divinity. The heavens show forth the glory of God, and the firmament declares the work of his hands."[2]

God comes to us in ordinary things.

Summer is winding down, the temperature is moderating, the grass is growing greener. I love the late summer and fall seasons. The peach tree I planted two and a half years ago is heavy with fruit, albeit small peaches. But these smaller than average fruit are sweeter than you can imagine.

Our twin apple trees are likewise bearing heavily again, for the second season in a row. I've been careful to pluck off nearly a third of the fruit to improve the size on these McIntosh apples. Macs, when fresh and fully ripe, remain one of my two or three favorites. They conjure memories of pulling a fresh apple out of the Halloween bag in late October. Biting into that crisp, juicy fruit was a childhood delight. Even the smell is unique. I would dearly love to plant a Courtland apple one day, an east-coast variety that I sampled my early years in college. That memory comes with the smell of salt air and seagull cries.

It's hard to describe the physical and emotional connection I feel to a tree I've planted, pruned, and harvest. I enjoy the process of care equally with the harvest. There is something about the time, the thought, and the effort that connect life and limb with the earth. I give to the tree—the tree gives back, and there is a cycle of giving and gratitude. As I care for my trees, my breathing slows, my mind centers and rests. I am forced to leave something of the pace and fragmentation of existence aside. Here, contentment is not elusive. Here, under a wide sky dotted with billowy clouds, it's easy to pray.

---

1. Dillard, *Holy the Firm*, 64–65.
2. Psalm 18:2.

Social Imaginary

I can only say that until you have done this, there is something of life and connectedness and grace that you don't experience. Part of the meaning of shalom is tied up in this relationship to land in the Old Testament, as well as something of the meaning of covenant. Husbandry is a good old word, and it applies equally to all kinds of care.

"In that day the Branch of the LORD will be
beautiful and glorious, and the fruit of the land
will be the pride and glory of the survivors in Israel." Isaiah 4:2

See also "Consumption"

SOCIAL IMAGINARY

I remember a scene about half way through the movie *Gandhi* where we see Gandhi and his family living on an Asram: a collective farm. The wife of this great leader is told she must clean the latrine and initially she refuses. A violent argument ensues where Gandhi shakes and slaps her. Then he realizes what he has done and asks forgiveness. She comforts him and then realizes what is at stake. Together they recognize what it means for human community when status is erased.

Somehow we have to get to the place where our function is not related to status. I think Jesus would have been okay cleaning the toilets, and my own need for importance is confronted by this scene in Gandhi.

We have sacrificed much to the god of efficiency. I, with my doctorate, am now most valuable as a writer/teacher so it is "inefficient" for me to clean the toilets. But is it really? If this new humanity God is creating recognizes something much deeper than function in our value before God, then maybe the most "efficient" way to teach something is not the words I use, but the way I live. The meaning of Jesus' sacrifice and incarnation turns upside down our cultural notions of value, of power and privilege. Love is inefficient, and weak and even foolish.

This may seem disconnected from the issue of culture and mission, but perhaps it's closer than we think. It involves living within the world where ordinary people live: entering their stories. We have tended to privilege the ministry of elites—those with plenty of education—who si-

Social Imaginary

multaneously resist getting their hands dirty. But if Charles Taylor is right that the intellectualized, trickle down view of cultural change is outdated, then we are really ready for his concept of a social imaginary, which is not a plausibility structure held by a privileged minority but rather resides in the stories and images held by common folk. Since lasting change will only come at that level, it's that world we have to enter. Hmm ... maybe the gospel stories show Jesus at all those common parties for a reason?

Newbigin envisioned an alternative plausibility structure to that of modern culture and it was based on a vision of local church communities re-engaging creatively and decisively with the narratives of Scripture.

> If we follow these suggestions we get a picture of the Christian life as one in which we live in the biblical story as part of the community whose story it is, find in the story the clues to knowing God as his character becomes manifest in the story, and from within that indwelling try to understand and cope with the events of our time and the world about us and so carry the story forward.[3]

In the last generation the formation of faithful communities was thought to involve primarily the formation of a Christian worldview. But while worldview thinking is critical of rationalist views of humankind, it still tends toward a cognitive picture of the person. Moreover, the pedagogies that have dominated the church have tended to reflect this approach. We have aimed primarily at forming the intellect.

But what if our hearts are not oriented primarily by an intellectual vision of the good life, but by our heart's grasp of it? What if we are molded and shaped by the rituals and practices of the mall and market, and our imaginations and assumptions are held there? Smith notes that the primary appeal is not to the intellect, but to the affections. It is not accidental that we are sold nearly everything we are sold in western culture through an appeal to sex or worth.

Smith argues that worldview thinking is reductionistic and has been misconstrued as the nature and task of formation because the operative notion of worldview was hitched to a misguided anthropology.[4] We need something more like Charles Taylor's social imaginary, a more integrative category than worldview that operates below the level of cognition. It assumes that we are embodied, and that our vision of the world is itself

---

3. Newbigin, *The Gospel in a Pluralist Society*, 88.
4. Ibid., 32.

embodied in images, stories and legends: held as much in our heart as in our head. Smith notes that Taylor is convinced that our focus on theory for understanding culture has been unhelpful—we must shift to the understanding that is embedded in practices.

He emphasizes that all societies and communities are animated by a social imaginary, but this does not mean that all are oriented by a theory. The social imaginary is much "broader and deeper than the intellectual schemes people may entertain when they think about social reality in a disengaged mode."[5] To call this an imaginary is already to shift the center of gravity away from the cognitive region to the affective—closer to the body. Imaginary thus hints at a more embodied sense of how we are oriented in the world—a noncognitive *understanding* rather than a cognitive knowing or set of beliefs.[6] "Our most basic way of intending and constructing the world is visceral and tactile—it runs off the fuel provided by the senses."[7]

No wonder the power of contemporary media! But there are also connections here to the tacit knowledge described by philosopher of science Michael Polanyi. There are many things we know that we cannot articulate. *The more you see, the less you know.* Knowledge is often held bodily, or by intuition, or within our senses. The mystics and poets have not forgotten this.

Smith makes the connection to liturgy—we are formed by what we worship.

> There is an understanding of the world that is carried in and implicit in the practices of worship and devotion. These rituals form the imagination of a people who thus construe the world as a particular kind of environment based on the formation implicit in ... such practices ... Christianity is a unique social imaginary that "inhabits" and emerges from the matrix of preaching and prayer ... Our precognitive disposition is love or desire ... and ... we love before we know.[8]

See also "Affections," "Epistemology," and "Narrative"

---

5. Ibid., 65.
6. Ibid., 65.
7. Ibid., 66.
8. Ibid., 70.

Theological Reflection and Theopoetics

THEOLOGICAL REFLECTION

Participative technology and the wisdom of crowds may hold more promise than we once thought. The need for theological reflection in a broader and open conversation and the possibilities offered was the driving force behind the Wikiklesia project, now almost two years distant. Reformation always demands theological work: The church must always be reforming. John Franke penned his paper from the classic position:

> Reformed theology is always reforming according to the Word of God in order to bear witness to the eternal truth of the gospel in the context of an everchanging world characterized by a variety of cultural settings ... In the words of Jürgen Moltmann, reformation is not a one time act to which a confessionalist could appeal and upon whose events a traditionalist could rest.[1]

Reaching further back, Karl Barth affirmed the need for the ongoing work of theology, firstly because theology is always human and limited. He writes that, "Theology is neither prophecy nor apostolate. Its relationship to God's Word cannot be compared to the biblical witnesses, because it can know the Word of God only at secondhand, only in the mirror and echo of the biblical witness."[2] If all theology is thus limited, it behooves us as a community of God's people to continue doing theological work. It may be that more light can be found today; that in light of a new situation we will see some issues with greater clarity.

---

1. Franke, "Reforming Theology," 1.
2. Barth, *Evangelical Theology*, 31.

Theological Reflection

In his primer in theology Barth tells a story about a series of lectures given in the postwar ruins of the Kurfursten castle in Bonn, Germany.³ Vigorous theological work is always done in the hope for a new world.

Elsewhere Barth comments on our proclivity for experts. In essence, he argues for the minority report. He had the wisdom to see that theological work is too important to be left for ivory towers. He writes:

> How disastrously the Church must misunderstand itself if it can imagine that theology is the business of a few theoreticians who are specially appointed for the task... Again, how disastrously the Church must misunderstand itself if it can imagine that theological reflection is a matter for quiet situations and periods that suit and invite contemplation, a kind of peace-time luxury... As though the venture of proclamation did not mean that the Church permanently finds itself in an emergency! As though theology could be done properly without reference to this constant emergency! Let there be no mistake. Because of these distorted ideas about theology, and dogmatics in particular, there arises and persists in the life of the Church a lasting and growing deficit for which we cannot expect those particularly active in this function to supply the needed balance. The whole Church must seriously want a serious theology if it is to have a serious theology.⁴

The theological foundations we work with were mostly built in modernity, filtered through Enlightenment lenses and limited by that context. The Enlightenment was the ultimate ivory tower. It presumed that we could stand objectively apart from the world and see through the pristine lens of reason. As a result, theological work was often overconfident and lacked a hermeneutic of finitude. We created an expert class of people to do the work for us. We forgot that experts are subject to their own distortions, isolating themselves into narrow conversations divorced from life as lived, and with the need to justify their own existence and privilege. Perhaps this was only another kind of power-play, another kind of colonialism. We have long assumed that theology done by western, European minds would be truer than theology done in other locations. This is why theologians like Kenzo Mabiala write,

> For many years, evangelicals have championed the cause of a self-theologizing Church, which they argued is the fourth woefully

---

3. Barth, *Dogmatics in Outline*, 7.
4. Busch, *Karl Barth*, 81.

needed addition to the classical three-selves of the indigenous Church (self-governing, self-supporting, and self-propagating). In postcolonial theologies, their dream has finally come true. The (subaltern) latecomer has finally spoken in her own native idiom. Evangelical faith, which has hitherto been articulated and formulated in the stable idiom of Western rationalism that guaranteed its sameness, suddenly finds itself confronted with other idioms that disturb both the stability of classical formulations and the appeal of sameness. Will evangelical faith break or stretch? Therein lies the question.[5]

See also "Empire," "Epistemology," and "Post-Christendom"

THEOPOETICS

It is at the level of the imagination that the fateful issues of our new world-experience must first be mastered. It is here that culture and history are broken, and here that the church is polarized. Old words do not reach across the new gulfs, and it is only in vision and oracle that we can chart the unknown and new-name the creatures.[6]

The term *theopoetics* was first seen in the form of *theopoiesis*, used by Stanley Hopper.[7] Since then, theopoetics has served as a noun referring to a particular devotional quality of a text, a genre of religious writing, and a postmodern perspective on theology. A useful working definition of the term would be the study and practice of making God known through text. Making God known through text? Surely this is a slippery adventure. But one of the main concerns of theology has been to bridge the complex world of experience with the story of God. Phil Zylla writes, "As experiences increase in complexity and depth the facility of language loses its capacity to express the hope of the gospel in relationship to the reality that we perceive and into which we attempt to live."[8]

---

5. Mabiala, "Evangelical Faith and Postmodern Others," 118–19.
6. Keefe-Perry, "Theopoetics," 579.
7. Miller, *Why Persimmons? and Other Poems*, 3.
8. Zylla, "What Language Can I Borrow?" 129.

Zylla references Donald Capps 1993 book, *The Poet's Gift*. Capps proposed that we consider poetry as a source of vision and inspiration for the pastoral task, and as a source of renewal for pastoral theology itself. In Capps view, both pastor and poet share a common passion for probing what is occurring beneath the surface. Both seek to understand the complex reality of human experience; both exhibit a deep care for words; both seek to ground reflection on actual situations; both seek to understand or pursue wisdom; both seek to write about the anomalies and tragedies and the unexpected blessings of life with thoughtfulness and passion.[9]

This is not far from James Smith's pursuit. While Smith is ostensibly pursuing a theology of cultural engagement, theopoetics pursues integration and honesty in the recognition that only whole persons before God will deeply experience the divine. Moreover, it is only as we invite others to live as whole beings before God that they will experience God in a meaningful way. We are embodied, and we live in a world of ambiguity in our daily experience: recognition of these realities is more likely to prove fruitful for a whole life spirituality than attempting to deny them.

Theopoetics isn't entirely new. Reading the work of Bernard of Clairvaux or William of Saint Thierry, one is dipping in an ancient stream, swimming along a different path of knowledge. This sacramental stream is founded on the love of learning and the desire for God. The monastic movement at its best, represented by people like Bernard or Francis or Benedict, or further west by people like Hildegard, Patrick, or Columba, was never about contemplation divorced from life in this world, but *as rooting and enabling life in this world*. These movements produced a great deal of poetry and prose, in the desire to share the fruit of the contemplative life. The love of learning and the desire for God converted men and women's bodies and souls so that all other loves became relative; or more precisely, all other loves were embraced for and through Christ and His passion.

Recently I picked up a novel that has sat on my shelf nearly thirty years—Charles Williams *Shadows of Ecstasy*. A day or two later, a copy of Smith, *Desiring the Kingdom*, arrived. As I browsed through the volume I came across Smith's argument that the erotic is precisely the lever we must reconsider in spiritual formation, so carefully employed by Hollywood and Madison Avenue. With our incipient dualism we have neglected this

---

9. Ibid., 130.

Theopoetics

area and left the door wide open for more secular aims. Smith notes the romantic theology of Charles Williams. Then a few days later we listened to Steve Bell in concert, telling the stories of his own growing devotion, rooted in people like Francis and in the great liturgical traditions.

Steve performed a number of his oldest compositions, including *Why Do We Hunger for Beauty?* As people hung on the words, and as the music brought water to our souls, I realized how hungry for God 'churched' people are. We dwell in the world of ideas, where the real is shadowed but not present. Appeals to the mind abound: but appeals to the soul, and our ability to live in that place, seem tenuous at best. We rightly recognize and are attracted to the beauty we see around us, but it too often becomes an end in itself rather than a path to something enduring. Beauty and love are ikons of the true: ikons rather than shadows, because shadow implies some lack of reality or something less than good. But beauty and love are not merely shadows or less than good, they are only less than God.

So we end with theopoetics, because after all there is no way to use mere words to describe the transformative power of love, any more than mere words can describe the lover's experience of the beloved. We use word-pictures and rhyme and music because poetry and music help words take flight, and the experience of love is both rooted and wild and words need wings to approximate it. We end up in the song of songs, or in the poetry of Saint John of the Cross.

> Your eyes in mine aglow
> Printed their living image in my own . . .
> Only look this way now
> as once before: your gaze
> leaves me with lovelier features where it plays.[10]

Smith hits it when he says that we become what we love. Worship in our Christian culture connotes bending the knee, but not always action in the world, and not always intimate connection. Smith has it right, but let me change the word to one that connotes worship but is less corrupt.

We become what we adore . . .

> I am my beloveds,
> And he is mine.
> He feeds his flock among the lilies.[11]

---

10. Nims, *The Poems of St. John of the Cross*, 20.
11. Song of Solomon 6:3.

Theopoetics

See also "Affections," "Epistemology," and "Social Imaginary"

Uncertainty

Uncertainty

I woke this morning from a dream where Bruce Cockburn was sitting at my table. He had huge Celtic sideburns, and it was as if he was there incognito. I recognized him and he laughed and said, "Yeah, well, I am supposed to be at this gig but really I just wanted a good conversation and a meal."

Lying in bed snuggling with my wife, appreciating the warmth of our bed while the house was cold, and the gift of the moment as I listened to the rhythm of her breathing ... I began thinking about leadership, and in particular that because we know so much less than we thought, the only way to lead in these times is to surrender. We must become great listeners, empty of our personal agendas. But the existing paradigm is all about dominance. What nut will buy this idea?

Certainty, in times of rapid change, becomes a commodity we seek. In times like these, we look for those who seem to know where they are going, even if they are only spouting yesterday's truth. When everything that can be shaken is shaking, we look for solid ground. When the system is disturbed it seeks a new equilibrium.

The virtues of uncertainty, then, are hard to extol. One of the most obvious to me is imagination, and, related, creativity. Liminality takes us to these places, because when our categories expand and old frameworks fail us, we have to seek and find a new synthesis. When the maps no longer describe the territory, we become seekers and learners. And that process, in turn, generates community because imagination and dreams are ill-defined places; they are wide spaces that invite participation. Imagination is thus a fundamental component of a creative commons, and these places of shared liminality are the only way forward.

Even such practical saints as Oswald Chambers had a deep appreciation for the power of holy imagination. Chambers wrote,

> One of the reasons for our sense of futility in prayer is that we have lost our power to visualize. We can no longer even imagine putting ourselves deliberately before God. It is actually more important to be broken bread and poured-out wine in the area of intercession than in our personal contact with others. The power of imagination is what God gives a saint so that he can go beyond himself and be firmly placed into relationships he never before experienced.[1]

The imaginative saint knows that mystery is as important as knowledge, and that to worship is to bow before a God who is totally other. We learn to honor the questions as much as the answer, because to be a disciple is to be a learner—one who is on a journey from the known, to the unknown. The imaginative saint is not fixated on the present order, as if this is as good as it gets, but knows that the eternal kingdom is a gift that is coming, and that gift is given to those who don't deserve it.

In recent years we in the western church have been enamored with certainty, and related, with propositions. As a writer, I understand the passion for words. As a lover, I am acquainted with their limits.

The dominant ways of knowing are one with the dominant culture. Epistemology is translated into an ethic. Since our primary way of knowing has been objectification, the direct application of power, our culture thrives on violence: Violence against women, against the poor, against our environment, against those who are too different from us. But what if knowledge has less to do with individual mastery and more to do with openness and community? Walter Brueggemann writes, "We all have a hunger for certitude, and the problem is that the Gospel is not about certitude, it's about fidelity."[2]

The fidelity of whom? Our standing before God is all about His faithfulness. He kept His promise in Jesus. We can now receive this fidelity through the living community, tradition (including Scripture) and the Holy Spirit.

---

1. Chambers, *My Utmost for His Highest*, 41.

2. Brueggemann, quoted at the Emergent Convention, Atlanta, Georgia, September 16, 2004.

Uncertainty

Does this mean we know with certainty? If not, then we are always left with some level of anxiety. Stan Grenz writes,

> We cannot simply collapse truth into rational certainty. Rather we must make room for mystery—as a reminder that God transcends human rationality. Central to the task of thinking through the faith is an obligation to rethink the function of assertions of truth or propositions. Christian truth is more than correct doctrine. Truth is both socially and linguistically constructed, and at the heart of Christianity is a personal encounter. Propositions may serve that encounter [but the map is not the territory].[3]

See also "Complexity," "Epistemology," "Liminal," and "Postmodern"

---

3. Grenz, *A Primer on Postmodernism*, 170.

Virtue

The great preacher and founder of the Methodist movement, John Wesley (1703–1791), was once approached by a man who came to him in the grip of unbelief. "All is dark; my thoughts are lost," the man said to Wesley, "but I hear that you preach to a great number of people every night and morning. Pray, what would you do with them? Whither would you lead them? What religion do you preach? What is it good for?"

Wesley gave this answer to those questions:

"You ask, what would I do with them? I would make them virtuous and happy, easy in themselves, and useful to others. Whither would I lead them? to heaven, to God the judge, the lover of all, and to Jesus the mediator of the New Covenant. What religion do I preach? the religion of love. the law of kindness brought to light by the gospel. What is this good for? to make all who receive it enjoy God and themselves, to make them like God, lovers of all, contented in their lives, and crying out at their death, in calm assurance, 'O grave where is thy victory! thanks be to God, who giveth me victory, through my Lord Jesus Christ.'"[1]

Not only do we seldom hear a question like this anymore, it's doubtful that many would offer an answer anything like the one Wesley offered. We don't talk about virtue these days,[2] and many who follow Christ are unclear about what the good life really looks like. Perhaps we are unclear about the goal of spiritual formation because we are unclear about who

---

1. Smith, *The Good and Beautiful Life*, 9.
2. I penned these words a few months before N. T. Wrights new book, *After You Believe*.

God is, and therefore what it means to be created in God's image. Wesley didn't have this problem. He knew that God was both Holy—and kind—both distant and totally other, and very near to us in Christ.

But perhaps there is a secondary reason that the gospel's *telos* has become obscure to us. In modernity the separation of secular and sacred, subject and object left us with a religion divorced from life in this world. Salvation became an other-worldly reality. Growth in grace was toward a future destination. How could we then value the virtues? The recovery of a kingdom theology and the rejection of a Gnostic dualism has made it possible for us to pray: Your kingdom come—on earth as it is in heaven; and mean it. Spiritual formation has become a process of shaping mind, heart and body for a celebration of life in this world.

See also "Foster, Richard," "Imago," " Formation, Spiritual," and "Social Imaginary"

W

Webber, Williams, and Wright

WEBBER, ROBERT

Bob Webber coined the term "ancient-future worship," and described it as rooting our worship in God's story, so that we embody not our culture but God's mission. Webber noticed the crossing of traditional boundaries and the growing interest in liturgy and the church calendar among diverse groups of Pentecostals and Evangelicals. He described it as tasting the communion of the fullness of the body of Christ. With this strong ecumenical interest, he was always inviting Christians to worship as one body, joined through "one Lord, one faith, one baptism."[1]

Webber was an American theologian, author, worship leader, columnist, and academic. He stirred up worship renewal by focusing on roots, connection, and authenticity in a changing world. For Webber, the road to the future was through the past. Born to Baptist missionaries, he graduated from Bob Jones University, earned degrees at Anglican, Presbyterian, and Lutheran seminaries, and taught at Wheaton College and Northern Baptist Theological Seminary. In *Evangelicals on the Canterbury Trail*, he chronicled his personal journey from fundamentalist to Episcopal Church membership (Anglican).

In the 70s, Webber's book *Common Roots* reminded Protestants that Christianity didn't begin with the Reformation. That's why he said it makes sense to study early church life, spirituality, witness, and worship—and see how it flowered from Jewish liturgical roots.

---

1. Ephesians 4:4–5.

To bridge biases, he persuaded evangelical leaders to jointly develop "The Chicago Call"[2] and "A Call to an Ancient Evangelical Future." Both documents argue for the need to connect with historic Christianity. Webber advised learning from "the entire worshipping community . . . liturgical worship, worship of the Reformers, the free church movement, Pentecostals, and charismatics."[3]

Webber developed a framework for looking at successive epochs of Christianity, each filtered through cultural principles that dominated in a specific era. "The story of Christianity moves from a focus on mystery in the classical period, to institution in the medieval era, to individualism in the Reformation era, to reason in the modern era, and, now, in the postmodern era, back to mystery."[4]

In one of his last books, Webber offered a taxonomy for the current ecclesial transition we are in. He described three types of evangelicals on the scene from 1950–2000: traditional, pragmatic, and the younger evangelicals (a term less value laden than *emerging* evangelicals). Under each heading he listed major categories like theological commitment, apologetics, and approaches to spiritual formation, worship, and evangelism. It was an attempt to map some changing territory and understand the landscape, something Webber was uniquely positioned to offer.

The book closes with a look at leadership in the twenty-first century. Perceptively, Webber understood a significant difference between established leadership and the younger leaders: "The new leadership is not shaped by being right, nor is it driven by meeting needs. Instead, it arises out of (1) a missiological understanding of the church, (2) theological reflection, (3) spiritual formation, and (4) cultural awareness."[5] His later work often had a prophetic ring.

Robert E. Webber died Friday, April 27, 2007 in his home in Sawyer, Michigan, after an eight-month struggle with pancreatic cancer. He was seventy-three years old.

---

2. 1977.
3. Webber, *Worship Old and New*, 21.
4. Webber, *Ancient-Future Faith*, 16.
5. Webber, *The Younger Evangelicals*, 240.

WILLIAMS, ROWAN

Why bring, to a contemporary conversation centered on culture, mission *in* western culture, gospel and ecclesial change, a Welshman named Rowan Williams, variously described as a poet, a theologian[6] with "two-brains,"[7] the 104th Archbishop of Canterbury, and thus a key leader in a mainline denomination with it's origins in a sixteenth Century conflict with Rome. After all, aren't so-called 'mainline' denominations in the west, dying? What might Williams add to the kinds of conversations described in the introduction to this emerging dictionary? There are a good many reasons why, but for the time being I want to offer two. First, his championing of mixed economies, mission-shaped and fresh expressions of church. When Williams addressed the National Anglican Church Planting conference in London on June 23, 2004, he introduced a term that reshaped how we think about being church in a range of different contexts, particularly in those contexts where the established model is that of a parish and a parish church serving its community.

Williams' talks about mission as finding out what God is doing in particular cultures and contexts and joining in. And, as a result of that work of discernment, we can begin to explore possible ecclesial responses to what we recognize God is doing in our cultural contexts. We can begin to creatively, imaginatively and prayerfully respond to Lesslie Newbigin's foundational question as to what would be involved in a missionary encounter between the gospel and western culture?

Williams expresses his commitment to the diverse expressions of church that might emerge as follows:

> We have begun to recognize that there are many ways in which the reality of "church" can exist . . . The challenge is not to force everything into the familiar mould; but neither is it to tear up the rulebook and start from scratch . . .

---

6. Along with his vast abilities as a theologian Williams is also a significant and important voice when it comes to the subject of Christian Spirituality. One of Williams' first books was *The Wound of Knowledge: Christian Spirituality from the New Testament to St. John of the Cross*. His deep understanding of (Christian) Spirituality (both east and west) is so important in our day when so many people describe themselves, to quote UK Sociologist Prof. Grace Davie, as *"spiritual but not religious."*

7. A description used by an Anglican Bishop friend to describe the fact that Williams is very bright and academically gifted.

> If "church" is what happens when people encounter the Risen Jesus and commit themselves to sustaining and deepening that encounter in their encounter with each other, there is plenty of theological room for diversity of rhythm and style, so long as we have ways of identifying the same living Christ at the heart of every expression of Christian life in common.[8]

Williams advocates for a both/and scenario, rather than an either/or one. We can have the "established" church and we can also make space for new and different ways of being "church" in response to our discovering *the* risen Christ and discerning his continuing kingdom-mission. In the U.S. these new or different ways of being church often fall under the amorphous umbrella of "emerging church," while in the United Kingdom these new ways of being church are popularly known as mission-shaped, or fresh expressions.

> Fresh expressions are a response to "our changing culture." This movement assumes that the church is shaped by both the gospel and the culture it is trying to reach. It is not meant to be conformed to culture, but it is meant to be appropriate for reaching and transforming a culture.[9]

Secondly, I want to highlight his recognition of the importance of becoming communities of diversity, commitment and shared practices in order to become more human, not less.

> "Catholic" and "evangelical" are words that belong together when they're properly used, because the good news isn't particularly good if it isn't the whole truth for the whole person.[10]

For Williams Christian spirituality, while centering on a triune God, is also profoundly concerned with us and with what it means to be fully human in community with others. These are important Jesus-shaped themes, which Williams keeps returning to time and time again. How are we to be fully human? And how is our becoming more fully human dependent upon the quality of our relatedness with others?

---

8. Archbishops' Council Report, *Mission-Shaped Church*, 2004, 7.

9. Cray in his report to the General Synod of the Church of England, February 2010.

10. Address to the Fresh Expressions National Pilgrimage, Coventry Cathedral, December 2008.

> In our feverish and impatient world, it is an important part of our Christian witness that we should be reminding people that our humanity needs time to grow, needs the time in which self-awareness, repentance and renewal can flourish. It is hard for so many to recognize that the path is a long one—that becoming human in God's way is a lifetime's matter. Yet the alternatives, so visible all around us, represent a trivialized and shallow humanity, anxious, angry and selfish, unwilling to look afresh at the self in the light of love and truth.[11]

And,

> [Saint Benedict's] Rule's sketch of holiness and sanity puts a few questions to us, as Church and culture. It suggests that one of our main problems is that we don't know where to find the stable relations that would allow us room to grow without fear. The Church which ought to embody not only covenant with God but covenant with each other does not always give the feeling of a community where people have unlimited time to grow *with* each other.[12]

And so, explains Williams, an important part of the attraction of the offer of Christianity,

> is living in a *larger* world, a world that takes human potential as seriously as God takes it. And I think that is in a world where often humanity *is* being shrunk and distorted by our systems and our ideologies and our politics, that sense of taking humanity with the seriousness God takes it and seeing that immeasurable possibility ahead of a joy that's continuous with God's own joy: I think that's worth believing.[13]

So, again, why bring Williams to the conversation? Well, of course for the two reasons already offered. But also, because of the contemporary rise of interest in mission-shaped church, because of our need and longing for genuine community, the interest in new forms of monasticism, increasing interest in spirituality, a recognition of the importance of rediscovering, recovering and re-contextualizing what is ancient[14]

---

11. Williams' letter to Prior Enzo Bianchi and the Community of the Monastery of Bose and all who attended the Seventeenth International Ecumenical Conference on Orthodox Spirituality held over the period September 9–12, 2009.
12. Williams, *God's Workshop*.
13. Williams, *Faith and History*.
14. For example, the work of the late Robert E. Webber in the USA, and the "deep

within our Christian tradition (east and west), and a longing for depth in an age of superficiality and Christianity-lite.

Williams, with his quiet-but-deep wisdom and learning, will be an important and needful conversation partner—particularly if what results from our questions and exploration is not to resemble the seed in Jesus' parable that falls on the path or on rocks.[15]

See also "Imago" and "Social-Imaginary"

WORLDVIEW (*see "Social Imaginary"*)

WRIGHT, N. T.

An attempt to summarize the contribution of people like Rowan Williams and N. T. Wright is ill advised. Alas, fools go where angels fear to tread.

Nicholas Thomas "Tom" Wright is the Bishop of Durham in the Church of England and a leading New Testament scholar. He is associated with the third quest for the historical Jesus and the new perspective on Paul, a movement originating with the work of James Dunn and E. P. Sanders. Wright distinguishes himself from both these scholars, and his own views are more nuanced.

Wright argues that the current understanding of Jesus must be connected with what is known to be true about him from the historical perspective of first-century Judaism and Christianity. Within evangelicalism, Wright has been well received, particularly by those who identify with the emerging missional church movement. Some of his popular interpreters include Brian McLaren, but his influence is much wider.

He has welcomed the hearing he has gained from the emerging church, but noted that his commitment to historical and biblical foundations is not always shared by the emerging church.[16] Some representatives of the Reformed evangelical tradition have sought to dispute Wright's theology, particularly around the issue of justification by faith alone. He

---

church" movement in the UK (see especially *Remembering Our Future* by Walker and Bretherton).

15. cf. Matthew 13:3–9
16. Wright, "On Justification."

addressed this issue in writing and sought to further clarify his position in an interview with Inter-Varsity Press.[17]

In the interview Wright points out that the doctrine of justification was shaped as an answer to questions which were not Paul's questions, but which made sense in the late medieval era. At the time the great concern was righteousness, and how to acquire enough of it so that God would declare you "okay." Wright comments,

> In a sense what, say, the Westminster Confession does is to give the right answer to the wrong question, because the question Paul is asking is not, "How can you get enough righteousness so that when God looks at you he'll be happy with you?" but, "How can you be sure that you are a member of God's people, that your sins are forgiven, and that therefore you are part of the covenant purposes of God which, ever since Abraham, have been the way in which God was addressing and rescuing the world?"[18]

Wright notes that in contrast, when we read Paul and grapple with what he meant by the concept of justification we are back in the world of first-century Judaism. The questions were very different, such as "How is God faithful to the promises to Abraham? How has that come about in what Jesus Christ has done in fulfilling what God always promised?"

Wright has also contributed to the discussion on the authority of Scripture. The inerrancy position that evolved in the last generation among Evangelicals was thoroughly rooted in Foundationalism and excessively abstract. Moreover, it was framed in a way that stifled engagement. Both N. T. Wright and Rowan Williams have helped move the discussion beyond those earlier parameters. In an interview in the Wittenburg Door in December, 2007 Wright was asked how we ought to balance experience and Scripture. He responded that,

> As we read scripture, we struggle to understand what God is doing through the world and through us. The phrase "authority of scripture" can make Christian sense only if it is shorthand for "the authority of the triune God, exercised somehow through scripture." When we examine what the authority of scripture means we're talking about God's authority which is invested in

---

17. Ibid.
18. Ibid., 4.

Jesus himself, who says "All authority in heaven and on earth has been given to me."[19]

Wright is aware that words like authority come with all kinds of religious and cultural baggage. But when he uses it, he describes the way the word functions and implies that the previous debate was not helpful. He notes that words like authority act as portable stories, shorthand that enables us to pick up many complicated things in a tidy way—like a briefcase.[20] But the intention is to unpack the briefcase later and put those things to use. He mentions the benefit of fresh air and perhaps a hot iron. When we forget that the shorthand is just that, we risk reductionism and distorting the terms of the conversation.

Wrights books have had a great impact within the missional conversation in the past five years, in particular *Surprised by Hope* (2008). Wright's eschatology avoids the dualism that is common among evangelicals. In an interview in 2008 he comments:

> Because Jesus is raised from the dead, God's new world has begun. We are not only the beneficiaries of new creation; we are the agents of it. I just can't stop preaching about that, because that is where we're going with Easter.
>
> For me, therefore, there's no disjunction between preaching about the salvation which is ours in God's new age—the new heavens and new earth—and preaching about what that means for the present. The two go very closely together. If you have an eschatology that is nonmaterial, why bother with this present world? But if God intends to renew the world, then what we do in the present matters. That's 1 Corinthians 15:58! The line I often use—which makes people laugh—is: "Heaven is important, but it's not the end of the world." In other words, resurrection means the new earth continues after people have gone to heaven.[21]

See also "Gospel" and "Kingdom"

---

19. Garrison, "Heavy Theological Dude Mistakenly Talks to Us," 11.
20. Wright, *The Last Word*, 24–25.
21. "Wright on Resurrection," 4.

Žižek, Slavoj

Slavoj Žižek is a Slovenian philosopher and critical theorist. With the 1989 publication of his first book written in English, *The Sublime Object of Ideology*, Žižek achieved international recognition as a social theorist.

David Fitch employed Žižek to criticize and obviate some of the obscure yet destructive aspects of American Evangelicalism. In 2007 he wrote an article proposing four public figures as symbols of who evangelicals have become in American culture: George Bush, Bernie Ebbers, and Ken Lay of WorldCom/Enron debacles (both evangelical Sunday School teachers), and Jessica Simpson, daughter of an evangelical youth pastor. Fitch examines these figures in culture as symptoms of what drives evangelicalism itself. He uses "symptom" in a way influenced by Slavoj Žižek. Fitch writes,

> For Žižek a "symptom" goes beyond the popular psychological notion of an external sign which points to a disturbance below the surface of one's psyche. For Žižek, a Symptom . . . can work within a culture to expose an unfulfilled drive, the unspoken void around which that culture (its Symbolic order or even ideology) has been formed. An image, an explosion of media activity surrounding an event, *a popular movie*, a flurry of publishing can expose something hidden and unspoken that drives a culture's meaning system. What we see and hear on the surface may be compensations for what the culture itself lacks at its core. The good news here is that exposing these kinds of Žižekian symptoms in cultures like America and/or evangelicalism opens them up for change and transformation.[1]

---

1. Fitch, "Žižek and Evangelicals in America," 6.

Fitch applies Žižek to the shock and awe of the war on Iraq, to homelessness, and then to the obesity of southern preachers. The application sounds similar to the Freudian idea of repression and transference. And it connects strongly to James Smith's analysis of desire.[2] We find a way to deny parts of ourselves that then manifest in destructive and unexpected ways.

But there is also good news here. Fitch notes that exposing these symptoms opens them up for transformation.

As I pen these words, the movie *Avatar* has exploded onto the screen. Its popularity has been stunning, in spite of a storyline that is somewhat tired. And the popularity of this film has not been limited to those under thirty. A symptom has been exposed. What does *Avatar* expose about our culture's meaning system?

The storyline is a close mirror for *Dances with Wolves*, where the tired civil war soldier is posted to the frontier and goes native. But soon after his friendship with the tribe is cemented, civilization catches up with him and he finds himself caught between two worlds. He sides with the natives, but progress won't be stopped and the colonization of the west continues.

Similarly in *Avatar* the future soldiers find wealth on a new world, with only some "backward" natives standing in their way. The film has been criticized for a tired storyline, but it has appeal for the same reason. There is something universal and mythic about this story, repeated through the ages, and obvious on CNN. And the film is stunningly beautiful. Employing the latest digital 3D technology, the story unfolds over nearly three hours while the exotic and other-worldly jungle invites us into a world of both danger and harmony. We escape from the technological jungle by virtue of the technological jungle.

I believe that the "symptom" *Avatar* exposes is the loss of community and the loss of a sense of connection with the transcendent. But more than this, it is the loss of simplicity. We face overwhelming complexity and deep problems, with no obvious solutions. But it isn't just the complexity that overwhelms us; we no longer possess the vision of a better future. In *Avatar* the villains are obvious, and while the solution may not be easy, it is at least morally evident. Moreover, it involves the restoration of a harmony we fail to experience in the complexity, isolation, and pace

---

2. Smith, *Desiring the Kingdom*.

of our culture. *Avatar* appeals to our longing for something like simplicity, or maybe something closer to "original participation."[3] We long for the restoration of all things—we want to get back to the Garden. *Avatar* offers us a vision of something like *shalom*.

---

3. Barfield, *Saving the Appearances*.

Bibliography

Achbar, Mark. *Manufacturing Consent: Noam Chomski and the Media*. Montreal: Black Rose Books, 1994.
Aelred of Rievaulx, *Spiritual Friendship*. Translated by Mary Eugenia Laker. Kalamazoo: Cistercian Publications, 1977.
Alves, Rubem. *The Poet, The Warrior, The Prophet*. Philadelphia: Trinity International Press, 1990.
Archbishops' Council. "Mission-Shaped Church: Church Planting and Fresh Expressions of Church in a Changing Context." Church House Publishing, 2004.
Austen, Richard. *Hope for the Land*. Atlanta: John Knox Press, 1988.
Bailey, Jeff. "An Interview with Gordon Cosby." *Cutting Edge* Magazine 5.2 (2001) 4–8.
———. "The Journey Inward, Outward and Forward." *Cutting Edge Magazine* 5.3 (2001) 10–14.
Barfield, Owen. *Saving the Appearances: A Study in Idolatry*. Middletown, CT: Wesleyan Press, 1980.
Barna, George. *Revolution*. Wheaton, IL: Tyndale House, 2005.
Barth, Karl. *Church Dogmatics,* 4.1. Edinburgh: T. & T. Clark, 1956.
———. *Dogmatics in Outline*. San Francisco: Harper Perennial, 1959.
———. *Evangelical Theology*. Grand Rapids: Eerdmans, 1963.
———. "Letter to a Pastor in the German Democratic Republic." In *How to Serve God in a Marxist Land*. New York: Association Press, 1959.
Belcher, Jim. *Deep Church: A Third Way Between Emerging and Traditional*. Grand Rapids: InterVarsity, 2009.
Bellah, Robert, et al., *Habits of the Heart*. Los Angeles, CA: University of California Press, 1996.
Benner, David G. *Sacred Companions*. Downers Grove, IL: Intervarsity Press, 2002.
Bonhoeffer, Dietrich. *Letters and Papers from Prison*. Clearwater, FL: Touchstone Books, 1997.
———. *Life Together*. New York: Harper & Row, 1954.
———. "Stations on the Road to Freedom." In *Letters and Papers from Prison*. Clearwater, FL: Touchstone Books, 1997.
Bosch, David J. *Believing in the Future*. Valley Forge, PA: Trinity Press, 1995.
———. "The Structure of Mission: An Exposition of Matthew 28:16–20." In *Exploring Church Growth*. Grand Rapids: Eerdmans, 1983.
———. *Transforming Mission: Paradigm Shifts in Theology of Mission*. New York: Orbis Books, 1991.
Brueggemann, Walter. *Cadences of Home*. Louisville: Westminster John Knox Press, 1997.
———. "Covenant as a Subversive Paradigm." *Christian Century* (1980), 1094–99.
———. *Hopeful Imagination*. Minneapolis: Augsburg Fortress Press, 1986.

Bibliography

———. *In Finally Comes the Poet*. Philadelphia: Fortress Press, 1989.

———. *The Message of the Psalms: A Theological Commentary*. Fortress Press, 1984.

———. *The Prophetic Imagination*. Minneapolis: Augsburg Fortress Press, 2001.

Buechner, Frederick. *Wishful Thinking: A Theological ABC*. San Francisco: Harper & Row, 1993.

Buker, Bill. "Spiritual Development and the Epistemology of Systems Theory." *The Journal of Psychology and Theology* 31.2 (2003) 143–53.

Busch, Eberhard. *Karl Barth: His Life from Letters and Autobiographical Texts*. Philadelphia: Fortress Press, 1977.

Capon, Robert Farrar. *The Astonished Heart: Reclaiming the Good News from the Lost and Found of Church History*. Grand Rapids: Eerdmans, 1996.

Capra, Fritjof. "Creativity and Leadership in Learning Communities." (Lecture, Mill Valley School District, April 18, 1997).

———. *The Hidden Connections: A Science for Sustainable Living*. New York: Anchor Books, 2002.

Caputo, John D. *Philosophy and Theology*. Nashville: Abingdon Press, 2006.

Cavanaugh, William. *Being Consumed: Economics and Christian Desire*. Grand Rapids: Eerdmans, 2008.

Chambers, Oswald. *My Utmost for His Highest*. New York: Dodd, Mead and Co., 1935.

Christian Classics Ethereal Library, "A Spiritual Canticle of the Soul and the Bridegroom." Online: http://www.ccel.org.

Clapp, Rodney. *A Peculiar People*. Downer's Grove: InterVarsity, 1996.

Cray, Graham. Report to the General Synod of the Church of England, February 2010. Online: http://www.freshexpressions.org.uk.

Cron, Ian Morgan. *Chasing Francis*. Colorado Springs: NavPress, 2006.

Cronk, Sandra. "Discovering and Nurturing Ministers." *Festival Quarterly* (1989) 12–16.

Dankes, Frederick W. *Jesus and the New Age: A Commentary on St. Luke's Gospel*. Philadelphia: Fortress Press, 1988.

Deering, Dilts, et al. "Leadership Cults and Culture." *Leader to Leader*, 28 (2003). Online: http://www.pfdf.org/.

Deiterich, Inagrace. "Missional Church: Cultivating Communities of the Holy Spirit." Grand Rapids: Eerdmans, 1998.

Dennis, Moe-Lobeda, et al. *St. Francis and the Foolishness of God*. London: Orbis Books, 1993.

Dillard, Annie. *Holy the Firm*. New York: Harper & Row, 1977.

———. *Pilgrim at Tinker Creek*. New York: Harper Perennial, 1974.

Driver, John. *Community and Commitment*. Scottdale, PA, 1976.

Eagleton, Terry. *The Idea of Culture*. London: Wiley-Blackwell, 2000.

Edwards, Jonathan. "Religious Affections, 1746." Online: http://www.ccel.org.

Eliot, T. S. "Burnt Norton, II." *Four Quartets*. San Diego: Harcourt Brace Jovanovich, 1971.

———. *Four Quartets*. San Francisco: Harcourt, Brace, Jovanovich, 1943.

Ellul, Jacques. *The False Presence of the Kingdom*. Philadelphia: Fortress Press, 1971.

———. *The Technological Society*. New York: Knopf, 1964.

Evans, Stanley. The Church in the Back Streets. London: Mowbray, 1962.

Fitch, David. *The Great Giveaway*. Grand Rapids: Baker Books, 2005.

———. "I'm Willing to die for It versus The Bible is Inerrant." Online http://www.reclaimingthemission.org.

Bibliography

———. "Žižek and Evangelicals in America: A Proposal." Online: http://churchandpomo.typepad.com.

Foster, Richard, J. *A Celebration of Discipline*. New York: Harper & Row, 1978.

Franke, John. "Reforming Theology: Toward a Postmodern Reformed Dogmatics." *The Westminster Theological Journal* 65.1 (2003) 13.

Freeman, Andy, Pete Greig. *Punk Monk: New Monasticism and the Ancient Art of Breathing*. Ventura, CA: Regal Books.

Friesen. "Blog." Online: http://dwightfriesen.blog.com.

Frost, Michael. "Evangelism as Risky Negotiation." Online: http://nextreformation.com/wp-admin/resources/evangelism.pdf.

———. *Exiles*. Peabody: Hendrickson, 2006.

Frost, M., and Alan Hirsch. *The Shaping of Things to Come*. Peabody, MA: Hendrickson, 2003.

Fullan, Michael. *The Six Secrets of Change*. San Francisco: Jossey-Bass, 2008.

Galli, Mark. "A Life Formed in the Spirit." Online: http://www.christianitytoday.com.

Gardner, William H. *Gerard Manley Hopkins*. New York: Penguin Books, 1963.

Garrison, Becky. "Heavy Theological Dude Mistakenly Talks to Us." Online: http://www.wittenburgdoor.com.

Gibbs, Eddie. *Leadership Next: Changing Leaders in a Changing Culture*. Downer's Grove, IL: InterVarsity, 2005.

Goertz, Donald, L. "Three Key Issues Facing Local Canadian Churches." *Missional Voice* 3 (2009) 2.

———. "Tyndale Seminary, Toronto." Online http://www.forgecanada.ca.

Greene, Colin. *Newbigin to Where?* Online: http: www.sgmlilfewords.com.

Grenz, Stanley. *A Primer on Postmodernism*. Grand Rapids: Eerdmans, 1996.

Guder, Darrell L., Lois Barrett. *Missional church: A Vision for the Sending of the Church in North America*. Eerdmans, 1998.

Hall, Douglas John. "Confessing Christ in a Post-Christendom Context." Paper presented at the Covenant Conference, Atlanta, GA. 1999.

———. *The Stewardship of Life in the Kingdom of Death*. Grand Rapids: Eerdmans, 1985.

Hauerwas, Stanley. "What only the Church Can Do." Online: http://faithandleadership.com/multimedia/stanley-hauerwas-what-only-the-whole-church-can-do.

Hauerwas, Stanley, and John Swinton. *Living Gently in a Violent World*. Downer's Grove, IL: InterVarsity, 2008.

Hauerwas, Stanley, and William Willimon. *Resident Aliens: Life in the Christian Colony*. Nashville: Abingdon Press, 1989.

Haugheny, Jim. *The First World War in Irish Poetry*. Bucknell University Press, 2002.

Heider, John. *The Tao of Leadership*. Humanics Publishing Group, 1986.

Heisenberg, Werner. The Uncertainty paper, 1927. Online: http://en.wikipedia.org/.

Henry, Patrick. *The Ironic Christian's Companion: Finding the Marks of God's Grace in the World*. Chicago: Riverhead Press, 2000.

Hiestand, T. "The Gospel and the God-Forsaken." Paper presented at the Eastern Theological Society, 2007.

Hirsch, Alan. *The Forgotten Ways*. Grand Rapids: Brazos Press, 2006.

Hjalmarson, "Toward a Kingdom Theology: Ending Violence Against the Earth." Online: http://www.precipicemagazine.com/toward-kingdom-theology.html.

Hock, Dee. "The Art of Chaordic Leadership." *Leader to Leader* 15 (2000). Online: http://www.pfdf.org/.

Bibliography

Holt, Simon Carey. *God Next Door*. Melbourne: Acorn Press, 2008.

———. "Time Away." Online:" http://simoncareyholt.typepad.com.

Keefe, Perry. "Theopoetics: Process and Perspective." *Christianity and Literature* 58,4, (Summer, 2009) 579–601.

Koch, Kathy. *Finding Authentic Hope and Wholeness*. Chicago: Moody Publishers, 2005.

Kronick, Joseph G. *Derrida and the Future of Literature*. Albany: State University of New York Press, 1999.

Kuhn, Thomas. *The Structure of Scientific Revolutions*, 2nd ed. Chicago: University of Chicago Press, 1970.

Lane, Belden, C. *The Solace of Fierce Landscapes: Exploring Desert and Mountain Spirituality*. Oxford: Oxford University Press, 1998.

Leclercq, Jean. *The Love of Learning and the Desire for God*. New York: Fordham University Press, 1982.

Lohfink, Gerhard. *Does God Need the Church: Toward a Theology of the People of God*. Translated by Linda M. Maloney. Collegeville, MN: Liturgical Press, 1999.

Lowery, Brian. "N.T. Wright on Resurrection." Preaching Today Blog. Online: http://blog.preachingtoday.com.

Mabiala, Kenzo. "Evangelical Faith and Postmodern Others," In *A New Kind of Conversation*. Colorado Springs: Paternoster, 2006.

MacIntyre, Alasdair. *After Virtue*. Notre Dame: University of Notre Dame Press, 1984.

Mander, Jerry. "Eleven Inherent Rules of Corporate Behavior." Online: http://www.nancho.net/bigbody/corprule.html.

Martens, Elmer. *God's Design*. Grand Rapids: Baker Book House, 1981.

McKnight, Scott. "The Ironic Faith of Emergents." Online: http://www.christianitytoday.com.

McLaren, Brian, et al. *A is for Abductive: The Language of the Emerging Church*. Grand Rapids: Zondervan, 2003.

———. *Finding Our Way Again*. Nashville: Thomas Nelson, 2008.

———. *A Generous Orthodoxy*. Grand Rapids: Zondervan, 2004.

———. *The Secret Message of Jesus*. Nashville: Thomas Nelson, 2006.

McNeal, Reggie. *Missional Renaissance: Changing the Scorecard for the Church*. San Francisco: Jossey-Bass, 2009.

———. *The Present Future: Six Tough Questions for the Church*. San Francisco: Jossey-Bass, 2005.

Merton, Thomas. *New Seeds of Contemplation*. New York: New Directions Books, 1961.

———. *Woods, Shore, Desert—A Notebook, May 1968*. Louisville: Bellarmine University, 1982.

Middleton, Richard, J. *The Liberating Image: The Imago Dei in Genesis 1*. Grand Rapids: Brazos, 2005.

Miller, David L. "Introduction." In *Why Persimmons? and Other Poems: Transformations of Theology in Poetry*. Atlanta: Scholars, 1987.

Miller, Lawrence M. *Barbarians to Bureaucrats*. New York: Ballantine Books, 1990.

Morgenthaler, Sally. "Leadership in a Flattened World," in *An Emergent Manifesto of Hope*. Grand Rapids: Baker Books, 2007.

Murray, Stuart. "The End of Christendom," Paper presented at Global Connections Interface Consultation, 2004.

———. *Post-Christendom: Church and Mission in a Strange New World*. London: Paternoster, 2004.

Bibliography

Murray, Stuart, and Ann Wilkinson-Hayes. *Hope from the Margins: New Ways of Being Church*. London: Grove Books, 2000.
Nelson, Gary. *Borderland Churches*. St. Louis: Chalice press, 2008.
Newbigin, Lesslie. *Foolishness to the Greeks: The Gospel and Western Culture*. Grand Rapids: Eerdmans, 1986.
———. *The Gospel in a Pluralist Society*. Grand Rapids: Eerdmans, 1989.
———. *The Household of God*. Bletchley: Paternoster Press, 2003.
———. *The Open Secret*. Grand Rapids: Eerdmans, 1995.
Nims, John Frederick. *The Poems of St. John of the Cross*. Chicago: University of Chicago, 1968.
Northumbria Community. Online: http://www.northumbria.org.
Nouwen, Henri. "From Solitude to Community to Ministry." *Leadership Journal*. Spring, 1995. http://www.ctlibrary.com/le/1995/spring/5l280.html.
———. *In the Name of Jesus*. New York: Crossroad Publishing Company, 1989.
———. *Lifesigns*. New York: HarperCollins, 1983.
———. *Reaching Out: The Three Movements of the Spiritual Life*. New York: Doubleday Company, 1975.
———. "The Rule—Briefly." Online: http://www.northumbriacommunity.org/.
———. *The Way of the Heart*. New York: HarperCollins, 1981.
O'Connor, Elizabeth. *Journey Inward, Journey Outward*. San Francisco: Harper & Row, 1975.
"Organizational Life-Cycles and Management Styles." Online: http://managementhelp.org/org_thry/life_cyc/cycl_ldr.htm.
Pagitt, Doug. *Reimagining Spiritual Formation*. Grand Rapids: Emergent YS, 2003.
Palmer, Parker. *To Know as We Are Known*. San Francisco: Harper & Row, 1983.
Pascale, Richard T., et al. *Surfing the Edge of Chaos*. New York: Three Rivers Press, 2000.
Peck, Scott M. *The Different Drum: Community Making and Peace*. New York: Simon & Schuster, 1987.
Perriman, Andrew. "What is Post-Evangelicalism?" Online: http://OpenSourceTheology.net.
Peterson, Eugene. *Christ Plays in Ten Thousand Places*. Grand Rapids: Eerdmans, 2005.
———. *The Contemplative Pastor*. Grand Rapids: Eerdmans, 1990.
———. *Reversed Thunder: The Revelation of John and the Praying Imagination*. New York: HarperOne, 1991.
Pinnock, Clark. *Flame of Love: A Theology of the Holy Spirit*. Downer's Grove, IL: InterVarsity, 1996.
———. *Tracking the Maze*. Eugene, OR: Wipf & Stock, 1990.
Polanyi, Michael. *The Tacit Dimension*. New York: Anchor Books, 1966.
The Prayer Foundation, "Dietrich Bonhoeffer Pages." Online: http://www.prayerfoundation.org.
Quotiki. Online: http://www.quotiki.com/quotes/13653.
Raine, Andy. "The Rule—Deeper." Online: http://www.northumbriacommunity.org/.
Ramachandra, Vinoth. "Christian Witness in an Age of Globalization" (Leonard Buck Memorial Lecture, BCV, Melbourne, May 10, 2006).
Renovare. "What is Spiritual Formation?" Online: http://www.renovare.org.
Rohr, Richard. "Days Without Answers in a Narrow Space." *National Catholic Reporter*, February, 2002.
Rollins, Peter. *How (Not) to Speak of God*. Brewster, MA: Paraclete Press, 2006.

Bibliography

Rowell, Andy. "60 Theologians on an Ecclesiological Spectrum." Online: http://www.andyrowell.net.

Roxburgh, Alan. *Missional Church*. Grand Rapids: Eerdmans, 1998.

———. Fred Romanuk. *The Missional Leader*. San Francisco: Jossey-Bass, 2006.

Roxburgh, Alex. *The Sky is Falling*. Eagle: ACI Publications, 2005.

Rumford, Douglas, J. *Soul Shaping*. Wheaton: Tyndale House, 1996.

Russ, Dan. "Babel: the Fear of Humanity and the Illusion of Divinity." A speech to the Dallas Institute, March 29, 2000.

Sacred Texts, "Canticle of the Sun." Online: http://sacred-texts.com/chr/wosf/wosf22.htm.

Selmanovic, Samir. "The Sweet Problem of Inclusiveness," in *An Emergent Manifesto of Hope*. Grand Rapids: Baker Books, 2007.

Shults, LeRon. "Reforming Ecclesiology in Emerging Churches." *Theology Today* (2009) 15–32.

Sine. "We've Got Rhythm." Online: http://www.msainfo.org.

Smith, James Bryan. *The Good and Beautiful Life*. Downer's Grove, IL: InterVarsity, 2009.

Smith, James K. A. *Desiring the Kingdom: Worship, Worldview and Cultural Formation*. Grand Rapids: Baker Academic, 2009.

———. *Introducing Radical Orthodoxy: Mapping a Post-Secular Theology*. Grand Rapids: Baker Academic, 2004.

———. *Who's Afraid of Postmodernism?* Grand Rapids: Baker Academic, 2006.

Snyder, Howard A. *Decoding the Church*. Grand Rapids: Baker Books, 2002.

———. *Liberating the Church: The Ecology of Church and Kingdom*. Downer's Grove: IVP, 1983.

———. *Models of the Kingdom*. Nashville: Abingdon Press, 1991.

Spoto, Donald. *Reluctant Saint: The Life of Saint Francis of Assisi*. New York: Penguin Books, 2003.

Stock, Jon, Tim Otto, et al. *Inhabiting the Church: Biblical Wisdom for a New Monasticism*. Eugene: Cascade Books, 2007.

Suh, Joe. "Social Networking and the Long-Tail Church." *Voices of the Virtual World*. Wikiklesia Press, 2007.

Sussman, Cornelia and Irving. *Thomas Merton*. New York: Image Books, 1980.

Tan, Seng-Kong. "A Trinitarian Ontology of Missions." *International Review of Missions* 93 (2004) 279–96.

Tickle, Phyllis. *The Great Emergence*. Grand Rapids: Baker Books, 2008.

Tomlinson, Dave. *The Post-Evangelical*. London: Triangle Press, 1995.

Touber, Tijn. "Our Natural Instinct to Heal," *Ode Magazine*, 4, 6, 36-40.

Turner, Victor W. *The Ritual Process: Structure and Anti-Structure*. Chicago: Aldine Publishing Co., 1969.

Van Gelder, Craig. *The Missional Church and Denominations: Helping Congregations Develop a Missional Identity*. Grand Rapids: Eerdmans, 2008.

Vanhoozer, Kevin J. "Pilgrim's Digress," In *Christianity and the Postmodern Turn*. Grand Rapids: Baker Book House, 2005.

Walker, Andrew, Luke Bretherton. *Remembering Our Future: Explorations in Deep Church*. London: Paternoster, 2007.

Walsh, Brian, Sylvia Keesmaat, *Colossians Remixed: Subverting the Empire*. Downer's Grove, IL: InterVarsity, 2004.

Bibliography

Webber, Robert, E. *Ancient-Future Faith: Rethinking Evangelicalism for a Postmodern World*. Grand Rapids: Baker Academic, 1999.

———. *Worship Old and New*. Grand Rapids: Zondervan, 1994.

———. *The Younger Evangelicals*. Grand Rapids: Baker Book House, 2002.

Weil, Simone. *Gravity and Grace*. New York: Routledge Press, 1952.

Westmoreland, Mark. W. "Interruptions: Derrida and Hospitality." *Kritike* 2.1, 1.

Wheatley, Margaret. "Consumed by Either Fire or Fire: Journeying with T. S. Eliot." *Journal of Noetic Science*. (November, 1999).

Wikipedia. "Différance." Online: http://en.wikipedia.org/wiki/Différance.

———. "Gregory Bateson". Online: http://en.wikipedia.org/wiki/Gregory_Bateson.

———. "Noam Chomsky's Political Views." Online: http://en.wikipedia.org/wiki/Noam_Chomsky's_political_views.

Wikiquote. "Werner Heisenberg. Uncertainty Principle." Online: http://en.wikiquote.org/wiki/Werner_Heisenberg.

Wilder, Amos Niven. *Theopoetics: Theology and the Religious Imagination*. Lima, Ohio: Academic Renewal Press, 2001.

Willard, Dallas. "Live Life to the Full." *Christian Herald* (U.K.) April 14, 2001.

———. *The Great Omission*. New York: HarperCollins, 2006.

———. *Renovation of the Heart*. Colorado Springs: Navpress, 2002.

———. "Spiritual Disciplines, Spiritual Formation and the Restoration of the Soul." *Journal of Psychology and Theology* 26 (1998) 101–9.

———. "Stepping Into Community." Online: www.relevantmagazine.com.

Williams, Rowan. "Faith and History." (Lecture, Westminster Abbey, March 19 2008).

———. "God's Workshop." Paper presented at the 2003 'Shaping Holy Lives', a Conference on Benedictine Spirituality, Trinity Wall Street, New York.

———. *The Wound of Knowledge: Christian Spirituality from the New Testament to St. John of the Cross*. Lanham, MD: Cowley Publications, 2003.

Williams, Stuart Murray. 2004. "The End of Christendom." Paper presented to the Global Connections Interface Consultation.

Wright, N. T. *The Last Word*. San Francisco: Harper, 2005.

———. On justification: God's Plan and Paul's Vision." IVP Academic. Online: http://www.ivpress.com/title/ata/wright_qa.pdf.

———. "On Resurrection." Interview in *Preaching Today*, March 19, 2008. Online: http://blog.preachingtoday.com/2008/03/interview_with_n_t_wright.html.

———. *What Paul Really Said*. Grand Rapids: Eerdmans. 1997.

Yancey, Philip. *Soul Survivor*. New York: Doubleday, 2001.

Yeats, "The Second Coming." Online: http://www.potw.org/archive/potw351.html.

Yong, Amos. "Discerning the Spirit(s) in the World of Religions." In *No Other Gods Before Me?* edited by John G. Stackhouse (Grand Rapids: Baker Academic, 2001) 37–61.

———. "Radically Orthodox, Reformed, and Pentecostal: Rethinking the Intersection of Post/Modernity and the Religions. In Conversation with James K.A. Smith." *Journal of Pentecostal Theology*, 15.2 (2007) 233–50.

Zylla, Phil. "What Language Can I Borrow?" in *McMaster Journal of Theology and Ministry*, 9,129. Online: http://www.mcmaster.ca/mjtm/pdfs/vol9/articles/MJTM_9.7_Zylla WhatLanguage.pdf.

Bibliography

Recordings

Cockburn, Bruce. *Child of the Wind*. Nothing But a Burning Light. Toronto: Golden Mountain Music Corp., 1991.

———. *Dancing in the Dragon's Jaws*. Northern Lights. True North Records, 1979.

———. *Mystery. Life Short, Call Now*. Toronto: Golden Mountain Music Corp., 2006.

———. *Pacing the Cage*. The Charity of Night. Toronto: Golden Mountain Music Corporation. BMI, 1999.

Cohen, Leonard. *Anthem*. The Future, 1992.

Jackson, Peter. *The Two Towers*. New Line Cinema, 2002. DVD.

Mayer, Peter. *Holy Now*. Million Year Mind. Minneapolis: Blue Boat Records, 1999.

Newcomer, Carrie. *The Gathering of Spirits*. Philo Records, 2002.

Plumb. *God Shaped Hole*. Sell the Cow Music, 2000.

Shyamalan, M. Knight. *Lady in the Water*. Warner Brothers, 2006. DVD.

Strauss, Norm. *Beauty in the Mystery*. Prodigal Daughter. Fabrik, 1998.

www.ingramcontent.com/pod-product-compliance
Lightning Source LLC
Chambersburg PA
CBHW071330190426
43193CB00041B/1264